Staying Out of
TROUBLE
IN A
TROUBLED
FAMILY

Rose Blue and Corinne J. Naden

Staying Out of TROUBLE IN A TROUBLED FAMILY

Twenty-First Century Books   Brookfield, Connecticut

Blue, Rose.
Staying out of trouble in a troubled family/by Rose Blue
and Corinne J. Naden.
p. cm.
Summary: Case studies and interviews present ways to cope with life
in a troubled family, including such problems as drug abuse, divorce,
child abuse, alcoholism, disability, and adoption.

ISBN 0–7613–0365–0 (lib. bdg.)
1. Social work with teenagers—United States—Juvenile literature.
2. Socially handicapped teenagers—Counseling of—United States—
Juvenile literature.   3. Problem families—United States—Juvenile
literature. [1. Family problems.]   I. Naden, Corinne J.   II. Title.
HV1431.B58   1998
362.7—dc21   98–15625
CIP   AC

Published by Twenty-First Century Books
A Division of The Millbrook Press
2 Old New Milford Road
Brookfield, Connecticut 06804

Contents

Acknowledgments

The authors thank the following people for their invaluable input and insight: Dr. Lillian Gross, Great Neck, New York, psychiatrist in private practice and board certified in child and adolescent psychiatry; Emily Luckett, Children's Hospital, Boston, Massachusetts, clinical social worker and psychotherapist; and Dr. William Nathan, child-adolescent psychiatrist, member of executive faculty of career training program in child and adolescent psychiatry, Menninger Clinic, Topeka, Kansas.

Prologue

Are you part of a troubled family? Do you have an alcoholic parent, a sister on drugs, an uncle who is physically abusive? Do you live in a home where you just don't feel safe? Lots of young people today have such problems. They are real and tragic and part of modern society, but it may surprise you to learn that they're not new.

In the nineteenth century and even back in colonial days, young Americans often found themselves in a family with troubles very much like your own. There were problems with alcohol or physical abuse, for instance, way back then. Of course, there was a big difference in the way these problems were handled.

Take alcohol, for example. In early America an alcoholic parent, instead of being offered counseling, might have been thrown in the stocks. These were wooden structures with holes in them for a person's arms, legs, and/or head. Usually the stocks were stuck in the middle of town so everyone could watch the fun of someone being punished. Sometimes a child who disobeyed, perhaps in school, was tossed into the stocks as well!

Discipline at home was another matter. Years ago, children were generally thought of as "property," usually the property of the father. It was not only Dad's duty, but his very right, to see to the discipline of his children. That sometimes led to "sparing the rod and spoiling the child" and a good deal of abuse. Schoolmasters were given permission to thrash their charges with whips of all kinds. Believe it or not, there wasn't even one organization in the world that protected children until the New York Society for the Prevention of Cruelty to Children was established in 1874! It was the first of its kind anywhere!

Another sixty-four years passed before children were legally protected from overwork and abuse. In 1938, President Franklin Delano Roosevelt signed the Fair Labor Standards Act. Part of it said that kids under sixteen could no longer work all day long in mines or factories! As for protecting against sexual abuse, that would take even longer. The Child Abuse Prevention and Treatment Act (CAPTA) was not passed until 1974.

As you can see, it's taken a long time to uncover the problems that have been troubling youngsters in troubled families for generation after generation. And that's just the point of this book. The problems of troubled families may not be new, but today there is a big difference in the way they are handled.

The difference is *help*. And help is what this book is about. *Staying Out of Trouble in a Troubled Family* takes a look at some of the problems that can face today's American families. It says that, unlike children of years ago, today's troubled young people really can find solutions. Someone is there for you.

Perhaps you're facing one of the problems discussed in these chapters. From Washington State to Washington, D.C., from Mississippi to Montana, from New Hampshire to New Mexico, kids are trying to stay out of trouble in troubled families. And, frankly, it's not always so easy being a kid in modern-day America, trying to bridge those troubled waters when others around you seem to be drowning.

You may not have a family problem that is new, but with any problem at all, you have a big edge over your long-ago cousins. You can get help. No matter what the trouble, no matter how bad it seems, help is there for you. You just need to know where and how to find it. This book will help you to do that. It talks about kids who face serious, hurtful times. Perhaps their problems are much like yours. These young people found a way out of their trouble. They found help. You can, too.

CHAPTER 1
DRUG ABUSE

Meet the Mitchells

It was springtime and roses bloomed on the lawn of the Mitchell home in suburbia. Birds sang and crickets chirped. It was quiet and serene. It was also spring break, which for Cheryl meant that her older brother, Jason, was going to be away on a class field trip for one whole week.

Cheryl sat on the edge of her bed drying her nails. She stood up to look out the window when she heard a truck rattling into the driveway. Who was that? The sign said Cross Country Movers, painted in crooked but glaring red letters.

Cheryl's parents saw the truck, too, from where they sat on the side porch. Mr. Mitchell got up and walked toward it, figuring that the driver needed directions. Somehow, Cheryl had an uneasy feeling about this, so she ran downstairs and joined her father on the front lawn.

The back door of the truck swung open and Jason leaped to the ground. He casually waved to the driver, who backed down the driveway and drove off. A little unsteadily, Jason walked toward his father and Cheryl.

"Hi, folks," he called. "Hi, Mom," he said as his mother now joined the group. "Guess what, Mitchells? I'm home!"

Jason's voice sounded thick and singsong, far away although he was now standing right in front of them. His parents watched in puzzled shock.

"What is it, Jason?" his mother asked. "Are you sick?"

"Why are you home, son?" asked his father.

Cheryl was silent, but she was screaming inside as her parents stood there and asked silly questions. Couldn't they tell? Didn't they know what was going on? Don't you see that he's stoned? she thought.

Dr. Margaret Stern is a well-known psychiatrist in a large eastern city. She speaks about Cheryl and her position in the Mitchell family: Cheryl feels like the monkey in the middle. It's a common feeling with children in some families where there is a drug problem. Kids like Cheryl, who are caught between their parents and a sister or brother on drugs, are stuck in a terrible place. It's often a real struggle for them to get out from under. And as in any struggle, the innocent party can often get injured in the process.

"Why don't they see?" Cheryl said to herself over and over. "How can they not realize what is happening?" Yet Mr. and Mrs. Mitchell continued to ask questions of their son, Jason, expecting logical answers from a teenage boy who was obviously in no condition to answer them.

"Was there a problem with the field trip?"

"Was the weather bad?"

"Was the trip canceled?"

"Did something happen to the bus?"

Perhaps they felt that if they could get logical answers to these logical questions, everything would fall neatly into place, like the front lawn.

Instead, Jason Mitchell stood foolishly on the grass, then began to whirl in a strange, disconnected dance. His parents watched in amazement as his arms flailed about as he slurred the words to a country song. Although it was hard to understand him, Cheryl knew he was trying to sing the words to "Country Life," which says that country life is not for a city boy and the city boy has to head for the bright lights.

Cheryl figured that her brother had simply gotten tired of the field trip. He didn't care for country life, and he didn't care for camping out. So he found some pot, or whatever else was around. It probably wasn't hard to find something. He'd probably carried some with him in the first place.

After he got stoned, Jason had simply wandered away from the camp and hitched a ride with the first truck that came along. The driver, perhaps bored with his own company anyway, was somewhat amused by the slightly stoned, harmless-looking kid, so he took him right to his front door. And here was Jason, home again and high.

But that didn't last long. Now he walked unsteadily into the house, followed quickly by his parents, and up to his room where he crashed, fully clothed in his rumpled jeans and dirty T-shirt right on top of his well-made bed.

Cheryl figured he'd be that way at least until the morning. But she said nothing to her parents as they closed Jason's door and talked to each other in calm bewilderment.

"We'll have to call the trip leaders in the morning. Jason might be in trouble with them."

"Maybe not. After all, the trip was voluntary and it *is* spring break. It certainly was inconsiderate of Jason, but he did have a right to leave if he wanted to."

"I guess so, but maybe we at least ought to call Dr. Smithers tomorrow and have him see Jason. Something seems wrong with him."

Dr. Smithers had been taking care of the family's health problems for years. He was a smart man and a good doctor. Cheryl was sure he would quickly figure out what was wrong with her brother. But then what? What would her parents do? How would they cope with the fact that their perfect son was on drugs? How would they cope with a problem that Cheryl had known about for what seemed like forever?

Cheryl stood in the shadows silently thinking her thoughts as her parents discussed her brother. This was nothing new—her being in the shadows. She had always felt that she stood in the shadow of her big brother.

Jason Mitchell was bright, handsome, charming, and popular at school. Cheryl had always adored him.

She could always count on him, lean on him. He always took care of her problems when she was growing up, always protecting his little sister. When she went to school, she followed in his tracks if not in his footsteps. She really didn't mind being known mainly as "Jason Mitchell's sister." It was really a compliment; it made her special somehow.

Stern: Cheryl has always taken somewhat of a backseat to her brother. Both at home and at school. But she became too comfortable in that seat, as she now realizes. This often happens when a son or daughter has to care for an elderly parent. The person who was cared for now finds him- or herself in the strange role of caregiver.

When Cheryl discovered that her brother had a drug problem, she was immediately cast in the unfamiliar role of protector for her big brother. This happened the first time she sprayed the house with heavy-duty air freshener to cover up the smell of pot before her parents came home one evening.

"How did it come to this?" Cheryl asked herself as she watched her parents trying to make some sense of the peculiar antics of her charmed brother. "How did this happen to our family?"

Even as the question formed in her mind, Cheryl knew there was no easy answer. Life wasn't *Jeopardy*, it wasn't a TV show. She realized it would be easy, and also unfair, just to point to her parents and say, "This is your fault."

Stern: The Mitchells are a hard-working, upper middle-class family. The picture of the ideal family, in fact. Mr. Mitchell is a successful business executive, and Mrs. Mitchell is a teacher in the local elementary school. They are also very active in a host of community affairs—leaders in the PTA, the Citizens' Council, the volunteer ambulance service, and various charities. Everyone looks up to them, as people and as parents. During his growing-up years, this has made Jason feel that no matter how high he stretches, he can never reach his parents' level. He can never be bright enough or caring enough to satisfy them. It's not that they ever told him such a thing, but he has always felt that this was the message his parents were sending.

Cheryl doesn't feel that much pressure from her parents. Perhaps because she is the younger child, the baby in the family, so to speak. Or, sometimes, there is still a message of less pressure given to the girl in the family, particularly a younger girl. And Mr. and Mrs. Mitchell are so calm and logical. This is not a screaming family. Although it is somewhat expected that a young girl like Cheryl can cry or even yell when things go wrong, such is not the case for Jason, as the older child and as the young man of the family. That is the message Jason receives and the one he acts on. He keeps his feelings inside and pretends to be the perfect teenager to round out his perfect family. When he could not contain his feelings or his pretense any longer, he looked for release. He has found it in drugs.

After the field-trip incident, Cheryl felt somewhat relieved. Surely her parents would soon realize the truth of the problem, and she would no longer have to carry the burden of Jason's drug use alone. Now she would have two extra people to help her. She would no longer be sitting on this powder keg by herself trying to figure out what to do. Should she tell her parents? Would that be betraying her adored brother who had always protected her? Yet how could he get help if no one knew he had a problem?

Stern: Like any other kid in her position, Cheryl is torn. She goes back and forth searching for an answer at a dizzying pace and gets nowhere. Now she feels that her parents will take the burden.

But when the smoke cleared, the Mitchells seemed to do more damage control than fact facing. They reasoned that Jason hadn't really gotten himself into any trouble at school because he bolted from the field trip. The Mitchells didn't lie—exactly—but they let it be assumed that their son had come home so quickly because he was ill. Actually, Cheryl figured that was not a lie at all, just a different spin on the facts.

At last, even Mr. and Mrs. Mitchell had to acknowledge that their son was in difficulty. And so, the entire family went to see Dr. Smithers, Jason alone at first, and then with Cheryl and her parents. As soon as they walked into the doctor's office, Cheryl could see that her brother was working the group in his usual assured manner. He hugged his mother's shoulder and smiled at his father, trying to charm his way out of the doctor's office and his problems. Cheryl could see that he wasn't leveling with anyone. When she tried to say so, she felt invisible and unheard. Once more, Jason was center stage.

Dr. Smithers seemed to fall for her brother's act, too. "Don't worry," he assured her parents, "Jason and I will have a few sessions together and get to the root of this problem. Experimenting in one's teens is not unusual. And drugs are so available these days, unfortunately. Still, Jason knows the worry he has caused you and the possible harm he can do to himself. We'll work it out together."

Well, maybe, Dr. Smithers *can* help, Cheryl thought as they left the office. And, true, over the next few days, Jason seemed to be more like the brother she had remembered from last year. He seemed untroubled and friendly. After spring break, he had returned to school with the "gee I had to come home from the field trip because I was ill" story. Jason was still the school superhero.

Back home, however, things had changed. Cheryl had a new position in the family. She was no longer the keeper of her brother's secret. Now she was the keeper of her brother. And she wasn't at all sure she was going to like it. "Look after your brother, Cheryl," her parents said. "We know he's trying to straighten himself out, but he's going to need some help and we often have meetings at night, so we can't be there all the time. We need you to keep Jason company. You know, talk to him, keep him occupied."

Cheryl knew exactly what they had in mind. Keep him off the drugs was what they were saying. Why me? Cheryl asked silently.

Jason regarded the situation as kind of a joke. "Hey, little sister," he mocked, "are you going to take away my key and hide it?"

Cheryl didn't want to take Jason's key, and she wasn't quite so sure she wanted to keep Jason in the family at all. When he was stoned—and, of course, it wasn't long before he was—he acted like some sort of weird Superman. He kept telling her he could fly and raved on about chartering a plane. He jumped from furniture to furniture, scaring Cheryl half to death with his antics. All this, naturally, when her parents were away doing good works somewhere else.

Before long, Cheryl began to sense that Jason was not the only reason her parents wanted her at home so much. If she were home, then they knew where she was. They began to question her in a way they had never done before.

"Where were you?"

"Why are you half an hour late?"

"Who were you with?"

"Where were your friend's parents?"

Even when Cheryl expressed interest in becoming part of her school's upcoming theater production, her parents were reluctant to have her be out of the house so much.

Cheryl began to resent her parents and her brother. Because of his antics, her behavior was now suspect as well. Were they looking for signs of drug use with her? Well, maybe she should give them a reason to be suspicious. She knew who had parties and what crowd in middle school served more than soft drinks. Maybe she should just join that crowd one night. . . .

Then, one evening Cheryl came home from play rehearsal to find a police car in front of the house. Jason was brought home with a warning about his strange behavior. The police didn't press charges, but they knew a family in deep trouble when they saw one. They had seen many kids in and out of drug rehab, ruining their school careers and their futures. "It's not too late," the policeman said to Cheryl's parents. "It's not too late for Jason if you start working at your problems right now."

Perhaps they really did see the seriousness of their son's drug use at last. Or perhaps they were just embarrassed by the police car parked at the curb in front of their manicured lawn. Whatever the reason, Cheryl's parents began serious sessions with Dr. Smithers along with Jason. But Cheryl refused to go. She wanted to see someone else, someone who would pay attention and would listen just to her. Dr. Smithers agreed and recommended Dr. Stern. It worked out well for Cheryl.

Jason was a popular sports hero both in middle school and high school. Through her talks with Dr. Stern, Cheryl began to see that she had to separate herself from her family to some degree right now, particularly her brother and his problems. Cheryl's talents lay in theater arts, an interest her parents didn't even know she had. Cheryl was encouraged by Dr. Stern to pursue those interests, to strike out on her own and find her own path. So Cheryl joined the school production and began going to rehearsals, even when her family would have preferred to have her at home where they could keep an eye on her and Jason at the same time.

Stern: Cheryl has to learn to be her own person, not Jason's sister, not the clone, not the monkey in the middle, but herself. She can continue to love and support her brother, but she cannot solve his drug problem. He has to do that himself. By following her own dreams, Cheryl can keep from following in Jason's footsteps and into deepening trouble.

Whatever the future for the troubled Mitchells, recently they had an especially happy evening as a family. Jason and his parents sat together in the Roosevelt Middle School auditorium and proudly watched a pretty good production of Shakespeare's *A Midsummer Night's Dream.* They were, however, even more proud of the playbill. It read: *Directed by Cheryl Mitchell.*

CHAPTER 2
DIVORCE

Meet the Alts

David Alt had looked forward to Thanksgiving Day for a long time. It was his favorite holiday. Especially this year. He loved the smells coming from the kitchen as his mother sang songs while she worked. He loved the way his father always made such a big fuss about carving the turkey just so. He loved having all his relatives around. It was a very special holiday for togetherness.

This Thanksgiving would be even more special, David decided. It had to be. Even so, he had crossed his fingers as the countdown to the holiday began. Although the weather was balmy and clear outside, clouds had gathered and darkened in the Alt household more and more during the past few months. The yelling sounded like thunder, and David had often buried his head in the pillow to block out the sounds in the night. But he couldn't block out the fact that he knew his mother and father were not getting along.

With the coming of the holiday would come a big family reunion to kick off the season. Everything would be better then, and the noises in the night would surely stop.

The turkey dinner was only the beginning of the wonderful year that David imagined stretched before him. Soon Grandma would arrive with her special baked-beans dish she made just for Thanksgiving. She lived down the block, and for months she had been the oasis in the desert. Grandma's was a place to run to when the sounds of battle grew too much to bear. She comforted David just as she had done when he was a baby, but she kept out of the problems her daughter and son-in-law were having. "They have to settle things themselves," she told David.

David knew it would be okay. It was Thanksgiving, and Grandma would be there. So would Aunt Jennie, Uncle Ted, lots of cousins, and Aunt Marge, Mom's best friend from childhood. David's sister, Melissa, would be home from college, too, for her first visit since she had started her freshman year.

David himself would graduate next June from Public School Number Six. And next fall, provided his grades remained high, he would be starting at Newton Tech Middle School. It was a new school, mostly devoted to science, and getting in hadn't been easy. But David had made it, and he had made everyone in the family very proud.

David also had a secret that, except for his parents, sister, and Grandma, no one else in the family knew. He had just been chosen to be master of ceremonies at his graduation from School Number Six next June. One member of the graduating class was picked each year for that special honor. His relatives would come from out of town to see him, he was sure, and perhaps spend part of the summer with the family.

Elaine Lester is a clinical social worker. She says that David feels he can keep his parents together. He will be the glue that holds the family in place. They will come together from far and near for his graduation day next June. If he just makes them proud enough, happy enough, the family will be together and his parents will stay together. That's a really tough job for an eleven-year-old kid. But like so many kids in troubled families threatened by a split, David cannot see that the job is not only tough but impossible.

Impossible or not, David had wished for a Thanksgiving Day just like always. And here it was. David felt he had made it so, made everything okay for this day, for the holiday season, for his graduation, for next summer, and on, and on, and on. . . .

Everyone did look comfortable and happy around the table. Well, everyone except Melissa. She didn't seem to be sharing the spirit of the day. She greeted her relatives, helped with the table setting, but she seemed to be more a guest than part of the family. Since she had gone to college, she seemed so far away.

Lester: Unlike David, Melissa has recognized the writing on the wall. She knows her family is in deep trouble and she is trying to distance herself, to protect herself from it. It's often necessary for a child in a troubled family to keep out of trouble by creating distance. But that doesn't work so well when the problem is divorce or separation. In that case, it's usually better to work things through as a family, if that's possible.

Melissa doesn't have to run away from home to get away from home. All she has to do is go to school, a few hundred miles away. She has always been the big sister that David counted on, and now that he doesn't truly know what parts of his life are solid, Melissa suddenly seems one less rock to support his world.

"Hey, little brother," Melissa said, "are you going to fight for a turkey leg?" She rumpled his hair and floated away into the kitchen. Her voice sounded phony to David, like a silly young actress on a bad TV sitcom.

"All right, everyone, I am about to carve this bird," Dad said in a voice that was too loud and too cheery, much like Melissa's. He adjusted his tall white chef's cap that he wore each year just to carve the turkey. Somehow, it didn't look as terrific to David as it usually did.

The family sat at the long table and watched the carving begin. Dad was expert as always, and the food, including Grandma's special dish, was perfect. Everyone chatted and laughed, and the family did seem to be having fun. David smiled. It was going to be okay. His thoughts drifted to next June and his graduation. Right after dinner, he would tell his relatives about his proud surprise. He pictured them all watching him as he hosted the graduation ceremony. Then he pictured them all at a big outside barbecue table. There would be lots of talk and laughter, lots of smiles and happiness, and lots of togetherness. Just like always, David was sure of that.

"Do you have a long break for the holiday?" Aunt Jennie asked Melissa. "Are you home for a while?"

Melissa paused a moment before answering. Finally she said, "Yes, school is closed for a while, but I'm going back on Sunday. I have a job working at the bookstore, so I've got to get back right away."

David was surprised. He hadn't heard about Melissa taking a job. In fact, he remembered that a few months ago his father had said he didn't want Melissa to work during her freshman year so that she could improve her grades.

"It's too bad you have to leave on Sunday," he said.

Now Dad spoke up in a quiet voice. "Speaking of leaving Sunday, I guess this is as good a time as any to make my announcement. I'll be leaving Sunday, too, leaving the house that is."

A strained and somewhat shocked silence followed. Dad cleared his throat and continued. "I'm sure it's no secret to any of you that Linda and I haven't been getting along. So, I'll be, as they say, fleeing the coop come Sunday. I've arranged to stay at a place near the office for the time being."

The fact that David's parents were having problems might not have come as a total shock to the relatives, but his father's announcement did. They sat in uncomfortable, strained silence, not knowing whether to put down their forks or continue eating. David looked at his mother, who seemed about to collapse on the spot. Finally she spoke.

"How could you do this?" she asked her husband from the other end of the table. "How could you make such an announcement like that in front of everybody? How can you make a joke out of this in front of the family? This is unbelievably insensitive, Martin, even for you."

David's father now looked uncomfortable. "I just thought it would be simpler," he said in a low voice. "Just to skip all the phone calls. This way there's no gossip or wondering. Just one clean break."

"You might have told me first," David's mother said in a bitter voice.

David stood like a stone statue. He couldn't believe it! He didn't even know his father was thinking of leaving, no less make an announcement of it right here around the Thanksgiving table surrounded by family!

What about his surprise? What about his graduation surprise? How could his father do this to him? Didn't he care?

David's mother ran upstairs in tears, with Grandma and Aunt Marge close behind. No one else knew what to do, so everyone just sat there, making awkward small talk and nibbling on cooling food.

Lester: This scene was totally devastating to David. Mr. Alt dropped a bombshell that rocked everyone. But why? Why then? His reason may or may not have been valid, but there is little doubt that Mr. and Mrs. Alt are in trouble. Martin Alt may need to question his behavior, and Linda Alt may need to ask herself just how she has contributed to this public disclosure at a family gathering. In addition, both of them must deal with how this impacts on their children, especially David, the younger child. No matter how painful it is, parents really need to explain a separation to their children, to let them know what is happening.

David had very little understanding of what was going on. All he really knew was that his entire world had exploded in his face. The Alt family would certainly keep this Thanksgiving Day in their collective memory. David was certain that his mother would never forget it, or forgive his father. As for David, it was a day he would remember with pain forever.

David lay in bed early Sunday morning listening to his father carrying load after load of luggage and boxes to the car in the driveway. He pretended that Dad was just going for a golf game as he sometimes did and would return a few hours later as usual. When he heard his father's car drive off, with Melissa in the front seat so that he could drop her off at the train station, David got up to face the day.

Mom fixed breakfast for him and made a small attempt at sounding cheerful. For his part, David ate what was in front of him, trying to keep the lump in his throat from gaining control. After all, he was the man of the house now, and he had to comfort and take care of his mother.

Somehow they got through the day, and the following morning David got on the school bus as usual, although in a fog. After school, however, he couldn't help but feel relief when he saw his grandmother standing at the front door as he returned home. He needed comforting himself, and she fit the part perfectly.

Lester: Adults don't always realize that parents are the most important people in kids' lives, and divorce is a wrenching loss to them, also. It takes time and help to get used to it and, it is hoped, to get over it.

Keeping your head above water in a divorced parent family is a problem shared, unfortunately, by many young people. The troubled waters are filled with swimmers. Take the year 1996, for instance. Some 2,339,000 couples married in the United States in 1996, and some 1,157,000 couples divorced. Using those figures, close to one of every two marriages in the United States will end in divorce. And an awful lot of those wrecked marriages involve children.

When two people marry, they usually discuss their future, how and where they will live, how they will raise their children, and other long-range dreams and plans. They very rarely discuss—except perhaps for the extremely wealthy who tend to worry over prenuptial agreements—what they will do if they split up. And they certainly almost never discuss how a divorce might affect their children. That's perhaps understandable. Who wants to talk about divorce on a day that you pledge to be together forever? To most people, divorce is unthinkable. It won't happen to me! Unhappily, and unfortunately for all, it does . . . to lots and lots of people.

When children are growing up, they generally feel, as David does, that the home will always stay the same. This thought and this feeling give children security. They also tend to feel that their parents are joined at the hip; they can never be parted. MomandDad is one word. But when MomandDad become Mom and Dad, it is hard to handle. The scene that took place at the Alt family holiday dinner was a ghastly drama for David to witness. But in one way or another, all such scenes, no matter how they are played out, are messy.

"What did I do wrong?" David asked his grandmother. "Did I make them mad? I know sometimes I forget to do stuff around the house. Is that why Dad doesn't want to live here anymore?"

Grandma tried to assure David that the trouble between his parents was not his fault. Grown-up problems are between grown-ups, she said, and David is still a child.

Lester: Children always feel that in some way they are responsible for the breakup of their parents. Then they go one step further, as David was about to do, and feel that it's their job to bring them back together—no matter what.

David is lucky to have his grandmother to turn to. If Grandma, or someone like her, is not there to help, a youngster should try to talk to a relative or family friend, someone whom he or she feels is best able to understand the situation on all sides. It's a jumping-off point that helps tremendously.

Grandma decided to try to bring the family together. Not to get David's parents back as a couple; she knew that her daughter and son-in-law must find a way to work out their own problems, no matter what the end result. But she did feel that Linda and Martin must come together to discuss their children. So she called and arranged for them both to come to her house along with David. Melissa was still away at school.

David fidgeted. He felt awkward. Dad tried to explain to David that it was best, at least for the time being, for him to be away from the house. "But no matter what happens in the future," Dad said, "we are still your parents. We always will be. I will always be your father and will always care about you, even if I'm not living at home."

Mom nodded. "We both love you and Melissa, David, and care about you as we always have. Even if we don't live together anymore."

David believed what his parents told him, but even so, the next few weeks and months were not easy. Dad came every Sunday as he promised and took David someplace special. That was nice, but it was strange. It was also strange for David's best friend, Allan. "I hate Sundays," Allan told him. "You're always gone, and now Bobby's on this divorce thing, too. I'm practically the only guy in the neighborhood with two parents home on Sundays, and I don't have anybody to hang out with!"

David said to his mother, "It seems so weird going to special places every Sunday. It's like every time Dad is with me, it's a holiday. It's fun, but it doesn't feel right. Before, Dad just used to be Dad; now it's like he's different somehow. It's like that book *A Month of Sundays* I read a long time ago for a report. The kid in the book was going through a divorce and he felt that way, too, about Sundays."

"Well, your father and you can stay here on Sundays if you like," his mother said. "That might make you feel better. It doesn't have to be special, and it doesn't even have to be Sunday."

Still David felt as though the pressure was building up inside him, and he didn't know how to handle his feelings. His grades began to slide by springtime. If this kept up, he knew he wouldn't get into Newton Tech after all. And he didn't even feel like rehearsing for his upcoming role as graduation host.

Grandma stepped in once again and decided that David needed a little extra help. "Come with me," she told him one day. "I want you to meet my friend Elaine Lester." She took him to a red brick building with a sign over the entrance that said: Senior Center, Junior Center, Family Center.

David knew that his grandmother spent time at the Senior Center. She had lunch there, took exercise classes, and swam in the pool every week. But he never knew that kids who had troubles, or who had gotten into trouble, went there, too. They helped the seniors who couldn't get around too well, and the seniors helped the kids with their problems. It was a satisfactory arrangement. Elaine Lester, a social worker, spent some time at the center as well. Grandma introduced David to her.

Lester talked to David for a while. "Sometime," she told him, "a person needs a little help from outside the family. Your grandmother is great, but she thinks it's best if you come to talk to me in addition. Is that okay with you?"

David liked Elaine Lester almost immediately and agreed to meet with her. Over the next months, she helped him to put the important things in his life into place.

> *Lester:* David's parents are trying their best to deal with a very upsetting situation for everyone. But in a split-up or divorce, the youngsters in the family must get to a place of healing and acceptance. It sometimes helps to talk to an outside person.

As time went by, little by little David began to come out of himself—to heal and to feel more relaxed and comfortable, although still sad, with the situation.

He began to do well once again at school, to feel less sorry for himself. Some of the seniors at the center had difficult problems too, and they were really gutsy. They had troubles he couldn't even begin to imagine. Slowly he began to see that if he kept on with a poor, poor David attitude, it could lead him down a road he did not want to travel. So, he decided that he would spend part of the upcoming summer working at the center, helping the seniors who needed help with their own troubles. In that way, maybe he could take his mind off his own.

Lester thought that was a wonderful idea, and she could talk to him at the center when he needed help. Even though David very much wanted his parents back together, he realized that such a thing might never happen. He knew that divorce was a very real possibility in his family. But he thought he could handle whatever came up.

It might not be such a bad summer after all, he decided. When graduation day arrived, there was nearly a whole row of the Alt family in front of him as he played the proud host at the ceremony. And best of all, thought David, as he held the microphone and welcomed everyone to his graduation, Dad was there. And it wasn't even Sunday.

CHAPTER 3
CHILD ABUSE

Meet the Denmonts

Miranda's face turned crimson. She felt flushed and uncomfortably warm in the cool of the late September morning. Today was the class trip to Lindenville Orchards. Ms. Hale was taking the group apple picking. They would select different kinds of autumn fruit, learning science, having fun, and enjoying raw and cooked apple desserts later on. Miranda had been looking forward to the day. It was her first year in middle school, and she was really enjoying it. Her teacher, Ms. Hale, was terrific. "You're doing great," she would tell Miranda, and Miranda could almost believe it. In fact, she was really beginning to feel that she was somebody—almost. Perky, never dull, all-around great teacher Ms. Hale could do that for you.

It was a perfect fall day in Linden, a small midwestern town south of Chicago. Miranda brushed her hair and pulled on jeans and a peacock blue, long-sleeved turtleneck. This seemed a good outfit for apple picking. Then she headed downstairs to wait for the bus.

"Hey," Uncle Carl called when she walked down the hall, "look at the blossoming young lady in that sweater! You sure are filling out real nice now. Growing up fast. I like it, Miranda."

Miranda didn't like it all, and she hated the sound of his leering voice. Despite herself, she felt her cheeks growing warm.

"Hey, you're blushing," Uncle Carl said with a broad smile. "It looks great with your hair. Come on over to your Uncle Carl." He rose from the recliner and began to walk toward her. Miranda backed up, but she wasn't fast enough. He grabbed her arm and, with his other hand, closed his fingers tightly over her shoulder. Miranda winced at the pressure. Then, he stretched out the collar of her turtleneck. "I think this is just a little too tight for you, Miranda, don't you agree?" he said with a low laugh.

Miranda tore away from him, nearly falling over the end table in the hall. Here it was barely eight A.M. and the day was ruined once again. As she ran upstairs, she could hear her uncle chuckling to himself. Back again in her room, she quickly changed her turtleneck for an oversized, baggy flannel shirt. Maybe her uncle was right, maybe that turtleneck was too tight for her. The shirt would hide her figure.

Actually, Miranda felt that she deserved to be punished many times during her young life. Practically from the moment she was born. From a very early age, Miranda realized that she was an unwelcome visitor into her mother's world. Mom, or Andrea, as Mrs. Denmont prefers to have her daughter call her, was only a teenager when Miranda was born and, in fact, still looks young enough to be Miranda's older sister. Her mother had been shunted from one foster home to another for most of her life. Andrea's father had been killed in an auto crash, and her mother had physically abused her, so the child-welfare agency in Chicago took her away and placed her into foster care. When she was sixteen, she took up with Anthony Denmont, a member of one of the local street gangs, and before long she was pregnant with Miranda.

At first, it seemed to Andrea that the pregnancy was really a blessing. Tony, who was nineteen at the time, actually seemed pleased at the prospect of being a father. And so, with the help of some of his less than legitimate contacts, they got some phony papers for

Andrea, and she and Tony were married. Andrea's life in foster care was over. She looked forward to a real home of her own and a brand-new future with Tony and their new baby.

The dream lasted just a few months past Miranda's birth. Tony Denmont was not in the running for father of the year. Bored with family life, bored with Andrea and a crying infant, he took off for parts unknown, leaving behind a photograph of a good-looking young man holding a newborn baby as Miranda's only tangible remembrance of a father. About three years later, Andrea got word from some of Tony's old gang members that he had gone to Los Angeles and had been killed in a robbery attempt.

Once Tony left, Andrea hadn't known what to do to take care of a crying, needy little person, who wasn't at all like the placid Barbie doll she had vaguely imagined. It wasn't enough just to dress and feed this little child. Miranda seemed to demand all her time.

Things improved a bit for Andrea and Miranda when they moved to Linden into the home of Andrea's Aunt Mae. She was a kind woman, who agreed to care for the baby while Andrea went out to work. Unfortunately, Aunt Mae was in poor health and died when Miranda was five years old. Since that time, Andrea had gone from job to job, and there was never enough money in the household. Although she was actually a good salesperson, she was never satisfied and never lasted very long in any one job. From time to time, a man would enter the house and stay a while. Miranda was told to call him "uncle." "Uncle Carl" was the latest and had been around for a few months.

However, with or without an "uncle" in the house, Andrea's feelings for her daughter remained the same. Miranda was constantly reminded in large and small ways that were it not for the burden of a child, Andrea Denmont would have one swell life. She could have finished school, even gone on to college, had a wonderful profession, and, of course, married a terrific and rich man.

> *Dela Cruz:* It's a common fantasy. In the adult's mind, it's not his or her fault, but the child's. Miranda is to blame for what her mother sees as her own no-way-out miserable life. The frustration of her failure to achieve the life she feels is her right is passed on to Miranda, and so is the abuse, like a family illness. That's the sad story with abuse; it becomes a family trait unless something is done to stop the pattern.

At various times, Miranda thought about the slaps that came from her mother over some slight or imagined wrongdoing. The memories came to her as she sat in class, fixed a meal, watched television, or walked down the street. She had gone to the grocery store a week before the class trip and passed a clothing store on the way. A rack of sweaters on sale was outside the store—no try-ons allowed. Miranda was carrying a grocery bag containing some breakable jars. Suddenly, a woman passing by swung as though to hit a toddler who was trying to pull over the rack of sweaters. The little girl flew toward Miranda, who stopped her with one hand, juggling the shopping bag with the other. The toddler clung to Miranda for a moment, then, a frightened look in her eyes, returned to the side of her screaming mother.

Miranda recognized that look and the feeling and the clinging to the mother who had just caused her terror and pain. She remembered so many scenes where her mother had lashed out suddenly for the most trivial of reasons. She remembered the hand reaching her head, her cheek, her stomach, sometimes causing her to fall to the floor. Now, running to catch the bus, Miranda remembered the little girl. It was the child she herself had been. Miranda was bigger now, but the scenes were much the same. Besides, now there was Uncle Carl.

But once Miranda was on the bus for the class trip, she felt better. Perhaps she could just forget about her home life for a while and concentrate on enjoying the day.

Ms. Hale sat next to Miranda on the trip to the orchard. She noticed the bruises on her neck. "Do you want to tell me what happened, Miranda?" she asked.

"It's nothing," Miranda replied with a shrug. "I just hurt myself. They'll go away."

Miranda didn't really lie to her teacher. The bruises would indeed go away, as they always did. But she just didn't tell Ms. Hale the truth, even though she liked her very much. Saying "it's nothing" wasn't really a lie either. To Miranda, the abuse was nothing unusual.

Ms. Hale was not the first teacher to notice Miranda's bruises. She was, however, the first teacher to ask Miranda about them clearly and directly. The teachers in elementary school had looked, frowned, and whispered among themselves, but they never asked, never spoke of them to Miranda or to the family. Now Miranda still was not sure how much Ms. Hale knew, and the young girl was so used to hiding and covering up that she just kept going that route on autopilot.

When Miranda got home from the trip, apples in tow, she was in a good mood. The house was empty, a great luxury. Miranda put away the apples, keeping some out to make applesauce. She peeled and cut the apples, mixed them with sugar and spices, and put them in a pot with water. She stood over the stove, stirring the apples and humming along with the kitchen radio as the smell of cinnamon filled the room.

Miranda never heard him come in. She was too engrossed in the music and her cooking. But suddenly Carl's hands were on her, moving to the front of her shirt. "The apples are as sweet as you are, baby," he whispered.

Miranda jumped back, the boiling sauce tipping from the pot and scalding her hand. Her screams mixed with her mother's voice. Andrea had just come in and saw that Miranda had knocked over the saucepan.

"Clumsy thing," she yelled. "You never do anything right. Never!"

If Andrea suspected or knew about her boyfriend's role in Miranda's life, she did not show it.

What did show the next day, however, were the burns on Miranda's hand. This time, Ms. Hale wanted direct answers.

Dela Cruz: Ms. Hale knew that thousands of battered children die every year—more than from accidents, drowning, or fire. The experts say that the number of abused children is at least three times more than reported, and thousands and thousands of cases are reported each year.

Abused children are not merely slapped by their parents or family members. Children can be abused in ways other than physical. They can be neglected or emotionally hurt as well. Mere words can cause terrible scars. Being told constantly that you are no good, worthless, unloved, and unwanted by an authority figure is serious abuse. After a while, a youngster begins to believe what he or she hears, and this can, and often does, lead to a life of failure and unhappiness. Miranda, in this case, is being abused in a number of ways, although the most pressing danger at the moment comes from Uncle Carl.

This time when Ms. Hale asked, Miranda told her teacher the whole truth and the story of her rotten home life. "At least it was step one," says Ms. Hale. "The abused child has to find the strength to reach out for help, and Miranda finally did."

Dela Cruz: If a child is too young or too frightened, an adult must often step in and save the victim. It can be a relative, a neighbor, a teacher. In Miranda's case, the teachers in her school did not want trouble, and so they looked away. Fortunately, Ms. Hale didn't feel that way. She read the signs and was willing to get involved. She came to me for help. Teachers and I often work together to help the kids.

One of Miranda's main problems was being told constantly that she never did anything right. Everyone needs to feel good about him- or herself. In this case, we had to show Miranda that what she did every day was very much okay. Her grades were good. She pretty much knew how to run a household at her young age. Miranda was also great with little kids and enjoyed helping in the day-care center next to her school. We had set up the center for teachers and other school employees.

But the very best thing that Miranda did was to turn to an adult she could trust—to save herself.

Ms. Hale and Rita Dela Cruz met with Miranda. At first, the young girl was far from cooperative for fear that police would come to her house and make matters worse. Eventually, however, her own need to turn her life around caused her to work with her teacher and the counselor.

Dela Cruz: When Miranda's mother was told of the situation with Carl, she sent him packing—much to Miranda's surprise.

Although her mother constantly told Miranda that she couldn't do anything right, she was really telling herself the same thing. She, too, had always felt that she was no good, and like Miranda, her mother had to learn that she deserved more in life, in Andrea's case more than a series of sleazy men who brought nothing but trouble.

A youngster like Miranda has a number of agencies, such as Families Anonymous or Childhelp U.S.A. (see *Where to Get Help* at the back of this book) that stand ready to give aid to those fighting problems of abuse. Third parties, such as neighbors, teachers, or relatives, also may turn to these organizations if they believe a child is being mistreated. The important thing is to get involved.

In Miranda's case, we decided that for the present we would try to handle the situation involving only Miranda, her mother, and the school. We now meet on a regular basis, and relations are improving in the household.

Miranda and her mother must come to think of themselves as a family, and that means they must learn to care for and respect each other. We must break the cycle of abuse so that it is no longer handed down to the next generation. To do that, we need to have Andrea stop the cycle so that it totally ends with Miranda.

Miranda continued to work after school at the day care center. She really enjoyed it. She felt as though she was giving something to the younger kids that she had never had when she was very young. She really felt that she wanted to make a difference in their lives. She told her counselor, "I want them to know that the sign over the day care center is true for them all. It says: At the Wee Care Day Care Center, We Really Care."

CHAPTER 4
ALCOHOLISM

Meet the Summerses

The volume on the television set was turned up so high that people passing by on the street could have heard it. Ted Summers didn't, however. He lay on the living-room couch, half conscious. All of his hearing and the rest of his mind had gone with the alcohol from the now empty bottle on the coffee table next to containers of take-out food.

Peter opened the front door and winced at the noise. He put his clarinet in the hall closet before walking across the room to turn down the volume. Then he surveyed a scene he had looked at countless times before. Maybe he shouldn't have stayed at school so late. Maybe he shouldn't be taking clarinet lessons at all, or going to rehearsals for the Harbor

High orchestra. If he stayed home, he might be able to keep things more in control and in order. Maybe.

The almost quiet seemed to nudge Peter's father into wakefulness. He struggled to a sitting position and began to fumble with the containers of rice and vegetables on the table. Peter could see his father's hands shaking as the food spilled onto the floor. Soon, another family member joined the scene as Sparky, Peter's dog, came running down the stairs.

Sparky began jumping up and down to catch the falling rice. The living room was a mess, and Peter tried to keep the dog from making it worse. Surveying all this was Peter's mother, now standing at the foot of the staircase.

Nurse Lynn: In spite of the fact that Mrs. Summers was in plain sight, Peter went right on trying to take care of the situation. It is his role. Like so many children of an alcoholic parent, he has become the caretaker. He never really thinks of doing anything but stepping in.

Peter moved to take the food containers from his father's hands. If he got the food away, it would end the spilling. Then he could deal with Sparky's eating habits and clean up the mess. Sparky, however, didn't quite understand the plan. He seemed to think that he and Mr. Summers were being deprived of a delicious snack.

"Down, Sparky," Peter ordered as he raised his left arm, holding a container out of reach.

Sparky ignored the order and went for the food. In doing so, his mouth closed, not on the container but on Peter's arm. The bite drew blood. Mr. Summers sat unmoving. Sparky barked loudly and then, seeming to understand what he had done, began to whimper. Mrs. Summers yelled from her position still at the foot of the stairs. Peter went to the bathroom medicine cabinet for some disinfectant.

His mother moved herself from the bottom of the stairs and followed him. "Oh, Peter, that's a bad bite," she said.

"It's okay," he told her. "It looks worse than it is. It's just a flesh wound. Sparky didn't mean it. He was just excited." Peter put his arm around his mother to reassure her.

Now Sparky entered the bathroom and lay down on the floor near Peter's feet. Peter bent down and patted his dog. "It's okay, Sparky," he said. "I know you didn't mean it."

Peter returned to the living room to clean up the mess. His mother came up behind him and looked at his arm. "That looks nasty to me," she said in a surprisingly firm voice. "And Sparky hasn't had his shots yet. I'm taking you down to the emergency clinic."

"It really isn't necessary, Mom, but if it will make you feel better, we'll go."

At the clinic, Dr. Miner agreed that it was a good thing Peter had come. "It's a nasty wound," he said, "but we'll fix you up good as new."

Peter shrugged. "It's no big deal."

"Well, it could be," Dr. Miner's nurse said. "By the way, I'm Lynn Brandopolis, but most patients just call me Mrs. Lynn."

"How do you do, Mrs. Lynn," Peter said politely.

"Better than you at the moment," she replied with

a smile. After giving Peter a tetanus shot and bandaging the wound, she walked to the door with him and his mother. "How did your dog happen to turn on you like that?" she asked casually.

"It was just an accident," Peter replied.

But Mrs. Summers burst into tears. "It was more than that," she cried. "I'm used to living this way, but now I'm getting frightened for Peter. What if he gets hurt badly next time there is trouble. He's so brave and grown-up for a thirteen-year-old boy. But still—"

Lynn drew Peter and his mother into a small room and sat down to listen to their story. When his mother was finished, Lynn handed her a card. "I spend a lot of time working with organizations that help families with such a problem," she said reassuringly. "They counsel the spouses and children. I'd like to see you both at a meeting next week, especially Peter." She gently put her hand on Peter's shoulder and turned him so that their eyes met. "You can't carry the world at thirteen, no matter how brave you are," she said. "Let me help. I've been where you are before you were born. I really can help. And so can this group."

Over the next few days, Peter tried to carry on as before. He tried to calm his mother, he walked Sparky, and he spent most of his time at school and in clarinet practice. Nobody at school asked what happened to his arm.

Lynn: Peter is a friendly boy. The other kids at school like him, but they don't know him very well. He never asks them to his home. He never encourages after school company because of his father's drinking. That's fairly typical. Most children of alcoholic parents are ashamed to invite friends to their homes. They feel embarrassed, and they try to cover up what they feel to be a terrible secret lurking in their family. What they don't realize is that their secret is shared by some seven million children in the United States. It's estimated that at least that many are living in homes where there is an alcoholic parent. If these children can be encouraged to attend meetings, they soon realize that they are not alone. For sure, Peter is not the only youngster in his town with such a problem.

Children of alcoholic parents are always worried about their home life. They're afraid that the alcoholic parent will get sick or hurt, or that they will hurt someone else. Peter has taken on an impossible job. Besides trying to keep things under control at home, he is keeping up his school grades. It's important to him to be part of the honors program at Harbor High. He is also on the school paper, in the science club, and part of the school orchestra.

Such activity is not unusual for children in Peter's position. They often tend to become overachievers. They take on the role of the responsible person in the family. In a way, they become parents to their own parents and grown-ups to friends their own age. But youngsters can push themselves only so far before they snap, like a stretched rubber band. Peter is on top of things for the time being, but it cannot last. Many children of alcoholics fail at school, get into trouble with the law, and begin drinking themselves. They feel guilty, that somehow something they did was the cause of the drinking problem. They feel hopeless, afraid they will wind up like the parent no matter what they do to prevent it.

Actually, it's true that children like Peter have to be on their guard. Alcoholism is an inherited disease. Studies show that if a youngster is born to an alcoholic parent but adopted in infancy by problem-free parents, he or she is still more likely than other kids to have problems with alcohol later in life.

Peter hardly remembered a time when drinking didn't play a large part in the life of the Summerses household. There were drinks at parties, at holidays, at almost any occasion. Glasses always seemed to be lifted in a toast to anything. It got so that Peter felt his father toasted anyone who just walked in the house to say hello. He began to think that his father saw the start of a brand-new day as the reason for a drink.

At first, though, it didn't seem so serious. It was kind of fun in fact, a sort of partylike atmosphere that would start as soon as his father walked in the door from work. But then Dad started to drink earlier and earlier in the day and later and later at night. He did manage to stay sober enough to work, but more and more he found excuses to work at home with his computer. That also gave him the opportunity to start drinking earlier in the day.

Peter also began to worry about his older brother, Ted, Jr. More and more, he seemed to enjoy lifting a glass with his dad. The younger Ted was away at college now, but Peter wondered and worried about him. When Ted, Jr., called home, all he talked about was the great campus parties.

Peter's arm got better, but he didn't forget about Mrs. Lynn, the nurse. Yet he didn't do anything about it either. In fact, he tried to put her and her words out of his mind. He told himself that he didn't need help. He was doing okay. The family was doing okay. Some days later, however, Mrs. Summers got a call from Mrs. Lynn asking her to bring Peter in so the doctor could check his arm.

After Dr. Miner pronounced him fine, Mrs. Lynn looked into Peter's eyes and said, "Your arm is healed, but what about the rest of you?"

"I'll be—" Peter began.

Lynn held her gaze and put her finger on Peter's lips. "Don't say it. Don't say, 'I'll be all right' and forget what brought you here in the first place. You can't forget it. And you will be all right. But not without help. Peter, I want you to come to tomorrow night's meeting. I want you to promise me that you'll come."

Peter kept his promise, and he attended many meetings after that. Sometimes he went with his mother. Sometimes he spent some time alone with Lynn. She became a safe haven for him, an adult he could trust, with whom he could be himself. As time went on, he began to learn a good deal about himself and his family.

Lynn: Peter began to let go a little, to loosen his grip on controlling his household. But letting go is very hard. I told him that he had to chill out, to detach himself just a little from his parents. He has to be a kid again, be himself. Be Peter, but just a little less than perfect.

As he spends more and more time at meetings with youngsters who share and understand his problems, Peter is able to relax a little. He no longer needs to cover up so much, to avoid, to keep everything inside. He can hang out without feeling weird about it.

Yet, it is not easy for Peter to stop carrying the world on his young shoulders. He has to learn that his father's problem is not totally his own. He has to learn that he is not the cause of his father's drinking. He didn't cause the problem, he can't control it, and he can't cure it. All he can do is learn to cope with it.

And so, little by little, Peter began to let go. He stopped trying to run everything at home and at school, or at least he tried to stop trying. He eased up on some school activities and concentrated on what he really liked best—the school orchestra and the newspaper. He found that giving more time to fewer activities made everything go more smoothly. It felt good.

Then Peter's brother came home from college for a few days. Peter wanted to spend some time with Ted, Jr., but his brother seemed to want to hang out more with Dad. One day Peter walked in from school to find the two of them drinking together. Dad was nearly drunk, and young Ted was obviously high.

55

Right away, Peter wanted to fix everything. It was Peter in charge once again, just like always. "What are you doing?" he yelled at his brother. "Do you want to wind up like Dad?"

"Lighten up," Ted, Jr., said. "We're just having a little drink." His speech was slightly slurred.

Angry, Peter reached forward to take away his father's glass. Mr. Summers raised his hand to his younger son. "Don't you dare disrespect your father," he said in a thick voice.

Peter ducked as his father's hand slapped at the air. Behind him, Peter heard his mother's voice. "And don't you dare raise your hand to any member of this family again," she said firmly.

Peter was startled. He had not heard such confidence in his mother's voice for a very long time. It sounded great. Mrs. Lynn was obviously helping her, too.

Tears welled up in his father's eyes. "I try hard not to hit my family," he said in a sad voice. "I don't ever want to get like that." He shook his head. "Not like my own father," he mumbled. "I never want to get like that."

> *Lynn:* Peter's father himself had been abused physically by his own father. So, Mr. Summers figured out that if he never got too near to his own children, there would be no chance that he would hit them. As a result, he hardly comes near them at all. He keeps his hands to himself, never touching his children, even with love.

Peter put his hand on his father's shoulder. "I know you wouldn't hurt me, Dad," he said.

His father smiled and blinked back the tears. Young Ted picked up his glass. "Hey, let's lighten up, everyone. Come on, Pete. Let's the three of us have a drink."

Peter thought about trying to stop his brother from drinking. Doesn't Ted see what alcohol is doing to their father, he thought? Was Ted going to become just like their father? What was going to happen to him?

> *Lynn:* Peter truly loves his father and his brother, despite their problems and lifestyles. But just as he can't control his dad's actions, he can't control Ted's potential problem either. He just has to step back a little and let his brother work on his own life. He can be there for Ted if he needs help, but he can't live Ted's life for him, or his father's. It's a hard lesson to learn at any age.

Peter looked at his father and brother. "I'll see you later," he said. "There's a square dance at the school tonight. Western food and country music. I'm going."

"A square dance!" Ted, Jr., laughed. "Why in heck would you go to that hokey kid stuff?"

Peter waved to his family as he walked out the door. "Because it's fun," he called. "Besides, I don't know about hokey, but, after all, I am still a kid."

CHAPTER 5
DISABILITY

Meet the Nortons

"Is he here?" Kathy rushed into the room calling, "Russell, Russell! Mom, is he here?"

Mrs. Norton raised the back of the velvet living-room recliner but didn't get up. "What do you mean 'is he here?' He's supposed to be with you. Where is he? It's snowing."

"I know it's snowing, Mom. It's windy, too. My boots are a mess. And that rotten Russell got away from me."

"Didn't you pick him up after kindergarten, Kathy? He's only five. You're the big sister."

"I *know* my job, Mom." Kathy answered hotly. "I'm in fifth grade. I pick up my baby brother from morning kindergarten. But he got away from me." Kathy said the last five words in a slow, exasperated tone. "We were coming through the park with about a zillion kids fooling around in the snow, and Russell just ran away from me. I couldn't find him, so I figured maybe he'd already come home."

At that moment, the front door opened and closed. Kathy turned to see Russell standing there covered with snow, dripping on the hall carpet. She rushed to him, not knowing whether to kiss him or hit him. She helped him off with his hat, mittens, and ski jacket. Then she saw the bruise just above his left eye.

Mom, still in the recliner, could see Russell in the hallway. Since he seemed to be all right, she asked, "Why did you run away from your sister?"

"Did someone hit you? What's that bruise?" asked Kathy.

Mom called for them both to come into the living room. "What happened to your eye?" she asked.

The picture of innocence in the face of all this questioning, Russell smiled and said, "I just wanted to play in the snow. I was just kidding with you, Kathy, but then I couldn't find you anymore so I came home. I can find my way."

"Don't you do that again, Russell," Kathy told him. "You scared me half to death. Don't you ever run away from me again."

"I didn't mean it," Russell said. "Anyway, Marco's dad came along, and he sort of walked us all home. After the snowball fight." Russell pointed to the bruise over his eye.

"What fight?" said Kathy. "Never mind. I get the picture. You got into a snowball fight and got the bruise. Right?"

Russell seemed pretty proud when he nodded yes. But Mom's voice was annoyed and accusing. "You could have hurt your eye or lost your eyesight. You're so careless. You don't take care of yourself, Russell. You just don't care about your health or anyone else's."

"Mom, he's only a kid. He was just having fun. I've got to get back to school. Lunch hour is almost over."

"But you didn't eat anything," Mom said.

"Don't worry. I'll pick up some milk and fruit. Russ's sandwich is in the fridge. See you later."

Kathy dashed out and back to school. She was wet, hungry, and upset. Sometimes she thought, as she rushed through the sloppy streets, sometimes she understood how Mom felt. Who needed Russell anyway?

Social worker John Sloan: That "who needs Russell anyway" attitude has rubbed off on Kathy. It comes from her mother. After all, kids learn from and imitate their parents. And whether or not Mrs. Norton realizes it, her message was coming through loud and strong—and unfortunately was reaching both her kids.

The next day the snow lay on the ground, mixing with ice, slush, and falling drizzle. At noontime, Kathy rushed to the kindergarten to pick up her brother. The teacher, Mrs. Crane, was zipping slickers, pulling on boots and caps, and watching out for parents to come for the children. Kathy figured you needed ten pairs of hands and eyes to be a kindergarten teacher. When she didn't see Russell right away, she decided to look around the crowded room before she panicked and bothered an already busy teacher.

Then she heard a familiar voice crying, "No fair!" It drew her into the lunchroom. A small group of four- and five-year-olds was standing in the middle of flying french fries and chicken nuggets.

Good thing there wasn't corn on the cob, Kathy thought, or else Russell would have a bruise over his other eye. Mr. Gelman, who supervised the lunchroom, pulled the little food fighters apart, and Kathy pulled a nugget from Russell's hair.

"You kids aren't supposed to be here," said Mr. Gelman. He was better with bigger kids and didn't really know what to do with squirming preschoolers. "Now get out of here and eat your own lunch."

Kathy left Mr. Gelman to deal with the others and led Russell out into the drizzle. They walked hand in hand, mitten in mitten. "Why can't you stay out of trouble?" Kathy asked her little brother. "You're always fighting. Yesterday snowballs, today nuggets. What next?"

"Joey started it," Russell explained.

"Sure he did." Kathy held on to Russell with one hand and opened the apartment door with the other. She wasn't about to let him get away again.

"What happened this time?" Mom asked from the recliner as they entered the apartment.

"Just a small food fight," Kathy said, and she helped Russell out of his gear. "Nothing major."

"More fighting!" Mom said with a sigh. "You both know that too much excitement is bad for my heart."

"It's okay, Mom. Nothing happened. Russell's okay."

"It was Joey's fault," Russell explained.

"I've got to get back to school, Mom," Kathy said. Once again, she had to skip lunch due to Russell's antics. She should have caught a flying chicken nugget in the lunchroom. At least she'd have had something to eat. Now she didn't know when she'd get some food. She had to go to the market after school, buy food, fix a midafternoon snack, and then start dinner. She didn't even have time to complain. Any stopping to chat would make her late for afternoon classes. She pulled on her mittens and headed back to school through the slush.

Sloan: Kathy has it rough for a fifth grader. She feels put upon and resents being saddled with so much responsibility at the age of ten. Yet, it has its perks being in her position. She gets to be a heroine, admired by her parents, friends, neighbors, and teachers. Children of a parent with a disability, such as Mrs. Norton's heart condition, often grow up quickly, mature well, and do well as adults, particularly if they serve as efficient helpers and can manage to control the resentment. It's an iffy situation, and Kathy might have gone either way. But poor Russell is another story. It's a sad story, and if nothing is done about it, Russell is in for problems.

Mrs. Norton had been a language arts teacher and librarian at a high school in the community. She had a reputation as an excellent teacher. Until Kathy was five years old, she remembered her mother as a perky, active woman handling job, house, and daughter. Outside of the fact that Dad's job kept him away from home a lot, Mom had it all and loved it.

Kathy was vaguely aware that her mother had a slight heart condition and that her maternal grandmother had died some years before of heart trouble. However, her mother didn't seem to be troubled by her problem, that is, until Russell was born. His birth left her with a disabling heart condition. She was forced to quit the work she loved and to curtail her activities sharply. Mrs. Norton blamed Russell's birth for her trouble and let everyone know it—often within Russell's hearing. She really didn't mean to hurt her son, but by the time he was old enough to understand, he was convinced that his mother wished he had never been born.

Late that afternoon, after food shopping, Kathy entered the apartment to find two neighbors, Mrs. Twersky and Mrs. Brodman. Russell called them the "borscht" ladies. Kathy thought they were angels. And the smells coming from the kitchen were wonderful.

"You must be soaked, dear," said Mrs. Twersky.

"Let me help put the groceries away," offered Mrs. Brodman.

"Thank you," said Kathy in relief. "Boy, am I glad to see you two!"

These two widows shared an apartment down the hall to save on expenses. The borscht ladies had become kind of grandmas to the Norton children. Kathy thought they were great and so did Russell. Russian borscht was their specialty, and it was heaven. So were their potatoes, chicken, and all kinds of delicious platters. They were always around, helping, bringing goodies into the apartment.

Kathy wolfed down hot borscht topped with yogurt and parsley. She felt warm inside and cared for. The cold was far away—for now. Once more, the borscht ladies saved the day.

The next day wasn't so great, however. Dad left for work early and couldn't take Russell to school. Kathy was late for her own class after dropping him off. She had had to help him get ready, and Russell was a dawdler.

Sloan: Kathy is becoming frustrated. She is starting to feel that she shouldn't have to do so much at home, and she isn't appreciated enough anyway. She thinks it's time that her family realizes that Miss Perfect doesn't have to be so perfect all the time. Then, maybe they will appreciate her more. Maybe even Russell will stop being a pain if he realizes that she can't always be around to keep him out of trouble. Maybe she'll just show them all.

Later that morning as Kathy headed for Russell's kindergarten class to pick him up, she passed the lunchroom and saw her friend Marie waving to her. She was unwrapping a calzone with mozzarella cheese, tomatoes, and all sorts of good-looking stuff.

"Wow, that looks great," Kathy said. She hadn't eaten a decent lunch in what seemed like years.

"Mom always gives me too much to eat," Marie said, holding out half to Kathy. "Take some. You'll be helping me to stay skinny."

"Thanks, Marie." Kathy bit into the delicious food. "That's great. Tell your mom thanks for me."

Marie laughed. "You should eat with us more often."

Kathy spent a few more moments enjoying the food and Marie's company. She rarely had a chance to do this. Russell could wait just a few minutes. Then the good feeling was replaced with a pang of guilt. With a quick thanks again to Marie, Kathy ran off to Mrs. Crane's class for Russell. But the kindergarten room was closed, dark, and locked. Where was Russell?

In a panic, Kathy rushed outside looking everywhere. After a couple of blocks, she spotted him leaving Oven Pan Pizza with Marco and his father. With great relief, she ran up to them. "I figured you just forgot the time, Kathy," said Marco's father. "So I took the boys for a snack, and we were just taking Russell home."

"Thank you so much, Mr. Aponte. I'm sorry I was late. I'll take Russell now."

So much for Kathy's rebellion, small as it was. No one would even know she had spent a few minutes talking to Marie.

Sloan: Kathy's attempted rebellion fizzled. It had no consequences except for her own guilt. A cycle of this kind of guilt and rebellion can be rough on young Kathy if she doesn't get some help. But still, the bigger problem

When Kathy and Russell returned to the apartment, Mrs. Norton was not on the recliner. Instead, she was in bed looking pale and having trouble breathing. "Russell," Kathy said in a shaky voice, "you go down to Mrs. Twersky's and ask them to come here. I'll call Dr. Hellman."

Russell was back with the borscht ladies in a few minutes. "Is Mom going to die?" he asked them.

"Of course not," Mrs. Twersky assured him, holding the boy close.

"Your mother will be fine," Mrs. Brodman said.

They were wonderful people, Kathy thought, but how did they know if Mom would be okay?

When Dr. Hellman arrived, he treated Mrs. Norton, left instructions for medication, and comforted Kathy and Russell. "Just a minor episode," he said. "A little rest and it will pass."

Russell was still trembling when the doctor left. He ran to Mrs. Brodman. "What will we do if Mom dies? Who'll be here?"

Sloan: Before kids are five years old or so, they see death as temporary. Like TV cartoon characters, people will die and come to life again. But later on, kids think about death more as grown-ups do. Yet, until they are about nine years old, they don't really grasp the idea that death can really happen to someone close.

The borscht ladies stayed. They helped Mrs. Norton, fixed snacks and dinner, and acted as grandmas to two very frightened kids. But it would take more than fixing food to fix the problems in the Norton family. And the two women knew it.

Sloan: It was time for more serious help, and Mrs. Twersky and Mrs. Brodman knew it. They suggested that Mrs. Norton do some tutoring in her apartment and in the building. It was a wonderful idea and a workable one. The borscht ladies spread the word that Mrs. Norton was available on a limited basis for tutoring. Before long, she had more customers than she could handle. This was work she loved, and rather than tire her out, it made her feel healthier than she had in a long time. Not everyone could pay for the tutoring, so in exchange the families offered services— food shopping, housekeeping duties, picking up Russell. This was great for everyone, including Kathy. But the family still needed more help.

And this was when I came in. Mrs. Twersky and Mrs. Brodman know my family well. We live just down the block. They know my daughter Alicia and know that she could use some tutoring. And they know I use a walker as a result of my automobile accident some years ago.

So, I've begun to counsel the Nortons as a family and also one to one. I also have a "families with disabilities" group meeting periodically in the Norton home. All the Nortons have begun to see how family members in the same boat cope with their problems. And they get to see me, a serious working, successful social worker who also has a physical disability. I must say, however, that no one enjoys seeing me as much as Russell.

All of the Nortons need help. Mrs. Norton needs help living with a physical challenge. Mr. Norton needs to quit hiding his head in the sand and burying himself in his work to stay away from an unhappy household. Kathy needs to let go, to be less burdened, to be free, to be a kid. Too much perfection at the age of ten is nothing but trouble.

But, most of all, Russell needs to know that his mother's illness is not his fault. As her life becomes happier and more productive, she will be able to show her son more attention and caring as well. The Nortons have a long way to go yet, but it's a start.

Kathy usually stays at school for lunch these days, hanging out with Marie and eating as many calzones as Marie's mother will fix! But sometimes, just for fun, she goes home for lunch.

One day she walked in the apartment to find Mom, Russell, Mrs. Twersky, and Mrs. Brodman sitting at the kitchen table.

"I'll set a place, dear," said Mrs. Twersky. "We weren't expecting you."

"Well, calzones are great," Kathy said, "but they're not like your borscht. And some days it's just good to eat lunch with the family."

CHAPTER 6
ADOPTION

Meet the Cormans

Sounds of music and laughter rang out at the Snowman in July rink. Noah had chosen this year-round enclosed ice-skating rink for his twelfth birthday celebration. Adam watched his handsome, athletic, tall, blond brother doing complicated maneuvers, balancing and twisting on one foot, then two, then one, looking casual and cool on the ice.

It was just like Noah, thought Adam, to choose the Snowman in July for his summertime birthday. To do something that got attention—an ice party in the middle of a long, hot summer. To do something that would show off his skills and get even more attention than he ordinarily did. And here was Adam, barely able to move on the ice, smaller than most kids at age ten, sitting on the sidelines unnoticed as his brother took center stage as usual. Everyone drifted off the ice, leaving Noah doing a solo on the rink. Then the applause came as he finished his performance.

Noah wanted ice skates. He got them. Noah wanted skating lessons. He got them. Noah wanted an ice-skating party in July. He got it. Adam lagged behind, head down as everyone followed the birthday boy to the Ice Fountain restaurant behind the rink. All Noah had to do was ask and he received. It wasn't fair. If Adam had been adopted, maybe he would get everything he wanted, too. After all, his parents had chosen Noah. When they had Adam, they had to take what they got.

Dr. Janet Lewis: When parents adopt a child, they often feel that the youngster is deprived to begin with, that the child will feel like an orphan, no matter what. In the case of Noah and Adam, where there are both adopted and biological children in the family, the situation becomes even stickier. The parents think that Noah will feel ever more deprived because Adam is their biological son. So they go too far in the opposite direction. The Cormans bend over backward to "make it up" to Noah, to make up for the fact that his biological parents gave him up for adoption. They give Noah too much, do too much, and it never occurs to them that Adam, their biological son, will feel second best.

The dining room of the Ice Fountain restaurant was decorated with a winter theme. Artificial snowmen, crepe-paper white bells, and snow scenes adorned the comfortably air-conditioned room. It looked nice enough to be a wedding party. There were burgers and chicken as at most kids' birthday parties. There was a snow-white frosted birthday cake with bowls of deep-red strawberries.

Noah stood up and walked to the huge cake. "Make a wish, birthday boy," someone shouted. Noah closed his eyes tightly and wished very, very hard. "I wish I knew my real parents," he cried silently. "I wish I knew my real parents."

"Blow out the candles," someone shouted.

Noah knew he had to snap out of his thoughts before the candles melted. He couldn't ruin the party for his friends. He was the star of the show.

Noah remembered the day about six birthdays ago when he learned what he had already suspected. He had come home early from first grade that day. The bus had dropped him off along with Adam, who was in preschool at the time. Mom hadn't remembered they would be getting out early that day because of a teachers' conference. The boys were greeted with loud voices when they entered the house. They both stopped at the hall closet as Mom and Mrs. Clarke argued in the living room. The boys didn't know whether to walk or go outside. As they stood in the hall, the words kept them glued to the floor. Although they knew it was wrong to listen to private conversations, they couldn't seem to move.

"Forget it, Jeanette," Mom said. "We go to church regularly, but I won't have anything to do with the so-called sisterhood."

"But why?" Jeanette asked. "I've been trying to get you to join us for ages. You're active in community courses and so are we. You'd be great. Why do you keep turning me down?"

Mom's voice was angry. "Because of the newsletter," she said.

"The newsletter?" Jeanette sounded puzzled. "What do you mean?"

"We were thrilled when we adopted Noah. I sent in a notice. It said that Mr. and Mrs. Corman proudly announce the arrival of their son Noah. Later, I found out that Martha Ross, the editor, wouldn't print it because Noah wasn't really our son at all but had been adopted because we couldn't have children of our own. I was furious."

"I can understand, Joan. But that was years ago, and Martha Ross has always been impossible. You can't judge the whole sisterhood by one person."

Noah felt as though his whole body had gone rigid. Adam dropped his schoolbooks, alerting his mother to the fact that the boys were standing in the hall. When Dad came home that night, Mom called a family meeting. The Cormans told their sons how happy they were when each of them came into their lives. Mom told Noah, "You grew in my heart. We wanted you so badly. We chose you." To Adam, they said, "We were surprised and delighted when we learned you were on the way. You grew inside mother in a different way."

Lewis: The Cormans said all the right things. But they said them later than they should have and in a way that was unplanned and shocking to both boys. If a child learns about an adoption accidentally, he or she will feel angry and distrusting of the parents. The youngster will think that being adopted is bad or something to hide and that his or her parents were ashamed, or else the adoption wouldn't have been kept a secret.

Actually, Noah wasn't totally shocked to learn he had been adopted. He couldn't put his finger on it, but at times he had felt different from the rest of the family, so the explanation was something of a relief. Also, nobody considered Adam's reaction. If Noah was chosen, what about him? Was he like a gift that you couldn't return if you didn't like it?

Noah smiled and waved to his friends at the birthday party. To everyone, he looked happy, but troubling thoughts kept flooding through his mind. Ten years ago, when he was born, who were his parents then? Why had they given him away?

Lewis: Noah's birthday thoughts are not unusual for adopted children. They fantasize about their natural parents being rich, famous, beautiful, and wonderful. They fear that they may have been given away because they were bad, or perhaps they were kidnapped. In Noah's case, his problem was deeper because he was followed by a biological child. He even thought that they had given Adam his name because he was regarded as the true first son. In actual fact, the Cormans just liked biblical names.

In this family, Noah needs help to understand his position more clearly and to air his feelings. Adam needs help as well to keep his big brother's role in the family from casting a shadow over his own life.

The Corman family soon became more troubled. A picnic was scheduled for the week after Noah's party. It was given by Adam's day camp and was to be held at a beach some distance away from town. There would be swimming and an outdoor barbecue. Since only kids Adam's age were involved, it was decided that Noah should spend that day with Grandmother Corman. Adam was kind of glad. He would get to have his parents for himself for a whole day. Besides, Noah didn't like outdoor picnics anyway. He was so fair that he always sunburned badly.

Lewis: Here is another reason that has made Noah sometimes feel he doesn't belong. He stands out so clearly from the rest of the family. Noah is tall. Both his parents and Adam are slightly below average height. He is very fair. The Cormans are dark-haired and dark-complexioned.

Noah didn't mind spending the day with his grandmother. She was warm and fun, and he never felt adopted when she was around. But early on the morning of the picnic, the phone rang. It was Grandma.

"Oh, dear," Mom told Noah, "Grandma has one of her bad sinus attacks. I'm afraid she doesn't feel well enough to have you go over there for the day. I'll call around and see whom you can spend the day with."

But it seemed that everyone else had plans for that day. "I'm sorry," Mom said to Adam, "but I'm afraid the picnic is off."

"I can hang out here alone," Noah said. "After all, I'm twelve now."

"No way," said Dad. "It's too long a day to leave you alone." He turned to Adam. "We'll have our own private family picnic. I'll barbecue in the yard."

"I'm really sorry, kid," Noah told Adam. He did feel sorry for his brother, who suddenly seemed so young.

Adam didn't blame Grandma. After all, it wasn't her fault that she got sick. "It's all your fault," Adam shouted through his tears at Noah. "He's always ruining everything."

Adam's feelings that Noah was the Corman family home wrecker, ruining everything, didn't end there. Soon after the party and the picnic that never happened for Adam, Noah came in carrying a large box.

When Adam asked what was in the package, Noah coolly replied, "New skates. The ones you got me weren't right. I'm just too good a skater for them."

His father overheard him. "Your mother and I thought those skates were fine. These look much more expensive. How did you pay for them?"

Noah shrugged. "I used the money Grandma gave me for my birthday."

His father frowned. "Noah, you know that money was for your savings account. You had no right to spend that without first talking to your parents about it."

Noah's face grew red. "My real parents would have given me the skates I wanted," he yelled. "You would have given me better skates if I were your real son."

Mom's voice broke. "What kind of talk is that? You know you're our son. And we thought we were giving you a fine gift."

Adam now joined in the discussion. "Why did you get him anyway?" he cried. "He spoils everything. He always makes trouble, and now he's made Mom cry. Why did you get him? Why didn't you just wait for me?"

Lewis: As Adam sees it, Noah is an intruder. An outsider brought into the family who does nothing but cause problems and throw the family group into a crisis. Deep down, Noah really feels much the same. He, too, feels like an outsider, different from the family. And so, the more the Cormans give him, the more proof he needs of their love. They simply cannot give him enough, however.

When Grandma heard of this crisis, she knew that the family needed a cooling-off period, so, when she felt better, she asked Noah to spend a few days with her. "You're getting so big, you'll forget about your grandma before long," she told him. "And with school starting soon, you'll have no time for me."

Noah laughed. "That won't happen, Grandma," he promised.

Hanging out with Grandma always made Noah feel better. She was an oasis in the middle of his family troubles. She was real, and nothing she said or did was hard to understand. Noah was her grandson, and he felt it was for real. He enjoyed her apartment complex, too. It was busy, bustling, humming with different languages and people of different ages. One thing everyone seemed to have in common was their affection for Grandma.

One afternoon at Grandma's, her friends Mrs. Marks and her daughter Nina came to visit. When Noah met them, he tried to stop staring. Mrs. Marks was fair and blue-eyed and Nina was dark, pretty, and clearly of Hispanic heritage. "Nina is adopted," Mrs. Marks told him. "I went to Brazil when she was an infant and brought her home with me."

"I'm sorry for staring," said Noah. "I hate it when people do that to our family. I'm adopted and I don't look like anyone either."

"You look like yourself," Grandma said. "That's good enough for me."

"I know your grandma feels that way," said Mrs. Marks, "and I know you're adopted, too. But believe me, we get lots more stares than you do. I just hate it when people say things like 'she's not your real daughter, is she?' She certainly is my *real* daughter and has been for eleven years. I took care of her, sat up nights when she was sick, and raised her. I better not hear that 'real daughter' business anymore."

Noah thought of his mother and that newsletter woman who wouldn't print his arrival announcement. His mother had been angry about that. She was always angry toward anyone who suggested Noah wasn't her real son. Looking at Mrs. Marks, Noah could understand how his own mother felt. Maybe he wasn't helping very much by always thinking of his own feelings. Yet the thought of who his biological parents might be still haunted him.

"Mom is my real mother as far as I'm concerned," Nina told him. "But I'm curious about my birth parents, too. In five years, Mom and I are going back to Brazil to see where I was born and find my biological mother."

Noah's eyes lit up. "Really? That's cool," he said. "I wish I could do that."

"Do you really?" Grandma asked. When Noah nodded, she took his hand. "Then, let's get your folks over and tell them that together."

This conversation involving Mrs. Marks and Nina led to the Corman family meeting with Dr. Lewis. She did a lot of work with adopted kids and their families, and she turned out to be just what the Cormans needed.

Lewis: All kids nearing their teens—adopted or not—struggle with identity. How they fit in the family. Of course, this feeling is stronger with adopted youngsters, who often need to know who their biological parents were. After meeting with me several times, the Cormans decided that when Noah was a little older, they would make every effort to find his birth mother and father. It helped Noah a good deal to hear that they were willing to do that. And it helped to bring the family together as more of a unit. Noah's troubles were rubbing off on Adam, as he, too, headed for his teens. Although our sessions were aiding Noah, Adam needed someone outside the family to listen to him, to really hear him. In time, this family unit would come together, but sometimes it takes a particular incident to show all the members what they really meant to each other.

Noah got home from school one day during the first week of the new term to find his mother pacing the floor. "Noah," she said, "I'm glad you're home. I called your dad. Adam wasn't on the school bus and he should have been home an hour ago. I'm worried sick. I've called everywhere. Can you stay here in case he comes in? I'll go out and look for him."

"Calm down, Mom," Noah told her. "I know Adam doesn't usually do stuff like this, but you stay here and let me go look for him. I'll take my bike."

"Thanks, dear," his mother said. "That's a good idea."

Noah threw his books on the table and rushed out for his bike. He knew where to look for Adam better than his parents did. And just as he suspected, he found his brother with a group of four other kids. They were lighting cigarettes behind the dumpster in the school yard.

"Okay, kid," he said to Adam. "Get rid of that and hop on the bike."

Adam was coughing too much to answer, but another kid spoke up. "Who are you telling us what to do? Get lost."

Noah got off his bike and towered over the kid. "You want to argue with me?" he asked. No one said anything. He took a cigarette from the kid's mouth and sniffed it. "At least, it's not anything worse than tobacco," he said. Then he turned to Adam. "Come on, kid brother. Let's head for home before Mom really flips out."

When Noah and Adam reached home, Mom ran to the door. "What happened? Where were you, Adam? You had me worried sick!"

Adam coughed again and tried to cover his mouth. "What's that smell?" his mother asked. She sniffed the air. "You were smoking! What's the matter with you, Adam Corman? You know better than that!"

Noah reached out for his mother's hand. "Steady, Mom," he said. "Don't you worry about the kid. It's just a phase, but it won't happen again. I'll take care of it, and I'll take care of him. It's about time." Noah put his arm around Adam's shoulder. "After all, what's a big brother for?"

CHAPTER 7
ALTERNATE FAMILY

Meet the Grants

The Card Carnival shop at Woodtree Mall advertised "miles of aisles." Wandering through the red carpeted greeting-card area, Amy believed it. The Father's Day section, for instance, was humungous. There was a huge assortment of Father's Day cards to Dad, as well as aisles and aisles of Father's Day cards to every possible male relative imaginable.

The Father's Day uncle cards were just across from the Father's Day father cards. Amy turned around so many times, she was beginning to feel dizzy. Should she get Uncle John a Father's Day card as though he were her real dad? Or should she get him an uncle card? She kept turning her head from side to side as though she were watching a tennis match. Then she grew tired of the card game and settled on two selections—one for her dad and one for Uncle John. Nothing, however, was settled in her mind. One card said, "to my favorite uncle on Father's Day." The other said, "to my father across the miles."

Reverend Joseph Moore: The greeting-card issue seems very minor, but it symbolizes a lot more than a commercial message from the marketplace to cash in on a holiday. The messages on the cards point up the confusion Amy has felt for so long. I've noticed that she sometimes calls Uncle John "Dad" and sometimes "Uncle John." I've also noticed that this is a little less of a problem regarding her Aunt Molly. Maybe it has something to do with the name. When Amy was little, the sounds of Molly and Mommy were similar. I have noticed, though, that she used the different names to let her aunt and uncle know her attitude toward them at any given time. When she is angry, for example, they are her aunt and uncle, not her parents. She has a natural dramatic streak—very creative. She reminds me so much of her mother.

Amy paid for the cards at the checkout counter. She wasn't sure she had enough money left after the purchase for blue nail polish, but she headed for the cosmetics area anyhow. Sometimes, when she was at the mall, she would spot a woman in the crowd who reminded her of her mother. Now, as she stood at the up escalator, it happened again. There, passing in a blink, was a very attractive woman with strawberry blond hair heading down the opposite escalator. Amy knew her mother only from photos in a family album, and, of course, she knew that her mother was dead. But somehow she felt that something of her mom's spirit remained, and so she watched for her.

Amy wished that she could remember her mother, to recall the laughing, full-of-life pretty woman who held her in those photographs. But the last picture of Amy with her mother, and of Amy and Mom and Dad as a happy family, was taken when Amy was only six weeks old.

Mom was thirty-three when Amy was born. One Saturday morning, nearly two months after the birth, Mom decided to go shopping to celebrate her newly regained figure. With Dad at home to watch the baby, Mom got an early start. She promised she would be home for Amy's next feeding, but she never made it. A drunken driver, going much too fast and returning from an all-night party, ran a light and crashed into Mom's car. She never had a chance.

Amy heard that story so many times from so many people through the years. Friends and neighbors had been stunned by the tragedy. Over time, people came to grips with the shock and went on with their lives. But Dad could not seem to get it together. Not then. Actually, not ever. A few years younger than his wife, he could not seem to rise to the occasion of raising an infant alone. Relatives and friends helped. They brought food and took turns caring for Amy, thinking that eventually Dad would get on his feet. But he never did, at least not to the extent that he could raise his daughter. His restless feet took him out of town, then home again for a while, and then off to another place. Now Amy was twelve, and her father was still wandering.

The first woman Amy called "Mom" was Aunt Molly. For a time, she also called Uncle John "Dad." At times, when Amy's father was in town, her aunt and uncle tried to be sure that Amy called her father Dad. But most of the time he wasn't there, so it didn't really matter.

When Amy was old enough to understand, she knew that her father's parents lived on the other side of the country. They seemed even less interested than their son in caring for a baby. And her own mother's parents were divorced, each with new families. They had no interest in turning their lives upside down with a new infant. So Molly and John, Mom's sister and brother-in-law, were elected to raise Amy. They had no children of their own, and Molly, who was fifteen years older than Amy's mother, had always shown interest in and affection for the child.

Now Amy's aunt and uncle were in their fifties, and as Amy grew older, she realized that the parents of other kids her age were much younger. Sometimes she got the feeling that her aunt and uncle were less than thrilled to be raising a child at this time in their lives. And sometimes she felt both sad and mad about that—like today when she couldn't quite bring herself to buy a "real" Father's Day card for Uncle John.

That night, Amy said at the dinner table, "Sunday is Father's Day."

Aunt Molly smiled. "Yes, and we're all going to the church lunch after services.

"Okay," Amy said. BORING, she thought. "By the way, I bought a card for Dad. Where is he now?"

Molly and John looked at each other. "We're sorry you spent your money," Uncle John said. "It was a nice thought, but right now we just don't know where he is. We haven't been able to reach him since Easter."

"He'll turn up," Aunt Molly said cheerfully. She didn't add what she was really thinking—like a bad penny—although Amy had heard Uncle John use that phrase many times when discussing her father. They couldn't fool Amy. She had always known that they rarely knew where her father was, didn't care, and never did approve of him anyway.

Moore: The Grant family has always had problems. The structure of a young mother's death, a disappearing and reappearing father, and older people who did not truly want the responsibility of a child at that time in their lives is far from ideal. Actually, if Amy's mother had lived, there may well have been trouble in the marriage. Amy's father has really never grown up himself. He was a handsome party boy who had trouble settling down to family life even before Amy's birth and seemed quite surprised to find himself with the responsibility of rearing a child.

So, in any case, Amy might well have been raised by her mother and a part-time father. Although she was too young to remember her mother as a person, Amy is aware that she has suffered a major loss. In a sense, she feels abandoned by her mother's death and abandoned by her father, who has gone off in search of himself rather than tending to his duties for his daughter. Amy never really had the opportunity to mourn her mother's death as she would have if she had been older at the time of the tragedy. You must mourn in order to heal. In addition, there is some friction now in the Grant home because raising a child has curtailed Molly's and John's freedom, even though they love Amy and will not admit to such feelings.

On Father's Day, Amy couldn't help but feel sad. Where was he? Was he thinking of her? Maybe he would call even though, on this holiday, she should be the one calling, or contacting, him. Amy reached out for the phone, but where would she call?

At breakfast before church that morning, Amy sat down at the table and wished her uncle a happy Father's Day. She gave him a hug, but she didn't say his name. It was true that he was the only father she had, the only game in town today. Yet she couldn't help feeling that he was just an understudy, and she thought that perhaps he felt that way, too. He was uncomfortable in the father role.

Amy handed him the Father's Day uncle card. "It's beautiful," he said. "Thank you." She also gave him the other one, but when he saw the "across the miles," his smile faded. He showed it to his wife and they exchanged glances. "You know, Amy," he said, "let's put this one away for your dad until we can send it to him."

Molly said nothing as they headed out to church, although Amy was certain that her aunt thought her skirt was too short. But Molly said nothing this time. She was aware that this holiday was hard on her niece, and she did not wish to cause further pain.

Amy fidgeted all through church services, a fact that did not go unnoticed by Reverend Moore. The church luncheon proved boring and the crowd dull. There were just too many fathers to suit Amy. Too many kids with fathers looking too happy.

So Amy left the church basement and headed for Dahlia's house. She was cool. So was her mother, who was a single parent. Nobody in that house would be celebrating Father's Day, and that was fine with Amy. When she got to Dahlia's, Evy was there, too. She **was** even cooler than Dahlia. Before long, Amy was decked out in green nail polish with small multicolored crescents. Then Dahlia's mother fixed them all some frozen pizza.

In the meantime, Molly and John were worried sick at home, wondering where Amy had gone. Just when they were about to call the police, the phone rang. It was Dahlia's mother.

"Amy doesn't know I'm calling," she explained. I think she just had to get away from things a bit today, but I didn't want you to worry."

"That's very nice of you, Mrs. Crawford," Molly said. "I know Amy thinks so much of you."

Mrs. Crawford laughed. "According to my daughter, Amy thinks I'm cool. I'm not really, but it's my cover and it works. This way I can keep on top of things without becoming my teenage daughter's enemy, if you understand what I mean."

"I think I do," Molly said, "and I'll keep your secret. Thank you for calling."

"I'll see that she gets home," Dahlia's mother promised.

The following Saturday Amy went to the mall with Dahlia and Evy. Amy watched in fascination as Evy wandered by the costume jewelry counter and casually dropped a pair of on-sale earrings into her pocket. How long had she been doing that? Amy wondered. Maybe cool Evy was just a little too cool.

On Sunday morning, Amy pretended a headache so she didn't have to go to services with her aunt and uncle.

Moore: When I saw Molly and John looking worried and Amy not with them, I spoke to them after services. It's been rough on the family, I know. I officiated at Amy's mother's wedding, baptized Amy, and six weeks later served at the funeral. It was a heartbreak. Although I asked Molly and John what the trouble was, I already knew. Amy is twelve, growing into the teenage years, and Molly and John are feeling out of their depth. They think her clothes are too daring, her makeup too much. She listens to loud music and sulks in her room. This is, in general, just growing-up stuff and not at all unusual, but in this alternate family, it is more difficult. No matter how much they love Amy and how willing they are to care for her, Molly and John are older than most parents of a child Amy's age. They hadn't planned on having any children at all, and now they find the teen years a problem.

I told Molly and John I would drop by the house that day.

Reverend Moore kept his word, and he told the family that he did individual counseling at the church center. He pointed out that many modern families do not fit into the mom-dad-children mode. Sometimes, these blended families need special counseling.

Amy commented that blended families sounded to her like yogurt, but she was willing to try. Her aunt and uncle agreed.

There were, indeed, many kinds of families at the Grants' church, just as there are in life. There are single parent families, stepfamilies, adopted children, families living together from two divorces, families with gay parents, and like Amy and the Grants, relatives raising the children. Molly and John were surprised at how many children were being raised by people other than their own parents, due to illness or drug problems.

Moore: Molly and John got a chance to air the toll that raising Amy was taking on them and their marriage. They are nearly senior citizens now, and John would like to retire, perhaps move to an adult community and relax. Molly feels that John resents having to raise his sister-in-law's child. But when everything came out in the open, the air became much clearer. The Grants know that they will never abandon Amy. They truly love her.

And Amy got to see many families in different situations and many youngsters in far worse family setups. She developed a respect and understanding for the sacrifices her aunt and uncle were making—willingly—and a clear view of the love that led them to such sacrifices.

One day after a counseling session with Reverend Moore, Amy walked in on what sounded like a scene from a bad soap opera. Her father, a pretty young woman with dark fuzzy hair, and her aunt and uncle sat in the living room talking loudly.

John said, "Martin, you can't think that Amy will be glad to see you. You should have seen her on Father's Day. She was miserable."

Martin replied, "I try my best. I come when I can."

"We're going to be married," the young woman chimed in, although no one had asked.

"I'm afraid I've heard that before," said John.

"Yes, this is real," Martin offered.

"Well, you're not," John replied. "We don't even have an address for you. What about Amy and this marriage?"

When there was no reply, Molly said, "When are you going to grow up, Martin?"

Amy stood with her hand on the doorknob. They hadn't heard her come in, and they wouldn't know if she left.

> *Moore:* Amy is about ready to run away again. Run from the family problems. She has been dealing with her losses alone, unsure about what was right, angry and resentful toward her family members. This is all quite common in a situation such as Amy's. But counseling is helping her to see that to heal you need to face facts. No family is perfect. In whatever situation, the family members need to support one another and try to work things through no matter what the particular crisis.

Amy slammed the door hard and stayed inside. She walked into the living room and hugged her father. "We're all glad you're here, really," she said. She turned to the young woman with her father and said, "Aunt Molly, don't we have some cake? Let's fix a snack for everyone."

"How long have you been standing there?" Uncle John asked.

Amy shrugged. "Not long. It doesn't matter. What matters is we're together now, and we're all going to sit down and eat."

"I'll help," the young woman offered.

Aunt Molly was silent. Everyone seemed on good behavior, and Amy seemed to be the new director of family harmony.

When her father and companion were leaving, Amy said, "Whatever you decide to do, Dad, I think I should have your address. I should be able to call you if I need you. What if someone gets sick? After all, you are my father."

Her father nodded but said nothing. Amy pressed on. "When will we see you again? Labor Day? Thanksgiving?"

"Christmas," her father said. "Before Christmas for sure. I promise. We'll get a tree and trim it."

"We have a tree," John said. "We use the ornaments we've used since Molly and I got married. It's a family tradition."

"Maybe we can add on to the tradition," said Amy. "We'll use some of our old ornaments and some new ones, too. Some brand-new ones for a brand-new family Christmas."

Her uncle laughed. "We might even pick out some orange, lavender, and pink ones, Amy!"

Aunt Molly smiled and patted her husband's arm. "What can you do, dear? It's tradition!"

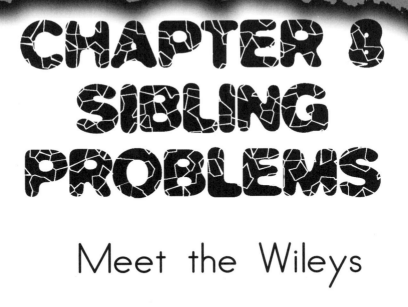

CHAPTER 8
SIBLING PROBLEMS

Meet the Wileys

Ten-year-old Tory kept hearing the words over and over again in her mind. It was as though a jingle for a TV commercial was stuck inside her head, and she couldn't shake it out. The words were always there: "You know I thought of having an abortion when I learned Tory was on the way."

It wasn't as though she had overheard something she shouldn't have. It wasn't that way at all. In fact, her mother had said those very words right in front of her! Mom was having one of "those talks" with Tory's older sister, Brenda, now thirteen, the other day. Tory was there, too. Mom seemed terrified that Brenda was showing interest in boys. She didn't seem to feel that

Tory was at that stage, but she didn't mind her over-hearing the lecture.

"You have to respect yourself and keep your distance," said Mrs. Wiley. "Most boys are out for just one thing. You have to be careful about whom you're seen with. Dating begins much too early these days as it is."

Actually, both Tory and Brenda had heard all this before, but on that day Mom added a new theme. As if to underscore the dangers of getting too close to those mythical creatures called boys, Mom said casually, as though she were announcing the menu was fish for dinner, "You know, I thought of having an abortion when I learned Tory was on the way."

Tory's mouth dropped open. "You didn't want me?" she gasped.

Her mother looked as though she hadn't noticed Tory was sitting there all the time. "Well, you know Brenda was only ten months old when I found out you were coming," she said calmly, lost in thought. "I really was shocked. It took such a long time before I became pregnant with Brenda that I never thought about having another child."

"Well, then, weren't two even better?" Brenda asked. Tory knew her sister was trying to put a positive spin on this conversation, but it wasn't working.

And Mom didn't help much. "Not really," she said. "You were so beautiful, Brenda. So sweet and such a good baby. You were so good that I thought I'd be able to go back to school, put you in day care, and finish my degree. Then I found out I was pregnant again. I didn't want to take another year off and postpone my career plans again. So I thought about abortion."

"Why didn't you?" Tory felt a little queasy just asking the question.

"Well, I decided it wouldn't be good for my health for one thing. Besides, I thought perhaps you would be a boy. You know, a girl for me, a boy for your father. I thought a boy would be someone for your father to go places with and leave Brenda and me alone."

That's a strange reason to want a child, Tory thought.

"Did Dad want a boy?" Brenda asked.

Mom shrugged. "Not really. He didn't care. Anyway, I don't know what I was thinking about. Weak as your father was, a son wouldn't have been any better. But no matter. Tory was born, and there sure won't ever be any more children for me."

Tory swallowed hard when she thought of that conversation. She had obviously disappointed her mother even before she was born. She had come along unexpectedly. She shouldn't have been born. At least, she shouldn't have been born a girl. The whole idea was so depressing that Tory left the house in tears and ran down the block to Aunt Kate's.

Aunt Kate Wiley: I was expecting this visit sooner or later. My sister-in-law was bound to let out her little secret to the girls. She isn't exactly tactful. Tory has been coming to me with her problems for some time now. I don't mind being sort of her second mother. Heaven knows she needs one. And my kids are out of the house now, so I have time and patience for my niece.

Tory sobbed in Aunt Kate's arms. "She didn't want me. She never wanted me. She still doesn't want me. She only wants Brenda."

"No, no," said Aunt Kate soothingly. "You know how your mother is. She doesn't mean half of what she says. She taught literature and drama so she gets a little dramatic herself at times. She just likes to feel a little sorry for herself, baby. All she really wanted was to impress upon Brenda that unwanted pregnancies should be avoided. And she's right, of course. She just got a bit carried away, honey, that's all."

Tory shook her head. "She never really cared about me, Aunt Kate. Not like Brenda. But I never thought she didn't want me to be born."

"Oh, no," said Aunt Kate, holding her tight. "We're all happy as can be that you're here. Your mother may be a little flowery in the way she speaks, but you bring joy to the whole family, Tory, and especially your old Aunt Kate. Now come on and have some tea with me."

Aunt Kate: I was a guidance counselor before I retired, but it's hard to counsel your own family. I guess I've been the aunt with Tory more than the professional. I tried to play down the abortion announcement, but it really was a bad scene for her. I don't understand it really. Myra married my late husband's brother when she was thirty. She wanted a baby so much that I think she would have married anyone. She certainly didn't seem crazy about Trevor. Five years later, Brenda was born. By that time, Myra had almost given up about having a child. But she was so wild about Brenda, you'd think she'd have been happy when she was going to have a second, but she wasn't.

I think the problem is that she never really wanted a husband. Just a child and a career. Now she's got two children, no career, *and* Trevor. I thought she'd leave him after Tory was born, but she's kind of put up with him and he doesn't seem to want to change things either. So they just sort of tolerate each other. But she certainly lays a heavy load on Tory with her abortion talk.

Tory always felt better after seeing Aunt Kate. But the good feeling lasted only a few days. Language arts was Tory's favorite class at school. She loved to read. She always got A's in that class, and Mr. Marone, the teacher, had high praise for his best student.

When her parents went to open school night with Tory, he said, "You must be very proud of your daughter. Tory is such a bright student, and her insight into literature at her age is really remarkable."

"She always was a bookworm," said Mom. "But a person should be well rounded. Was Brenda, her sister, in your class?"

Mr. Marone shook his head. "No, she wasn't, but I'm sure she was a good student, too."

"In everything," said Mom. "And she was always so social and active in other areas as well here in middle school. Now she's in Millville High, and we're very proud of her."

Tory's father finally spoke up. "We're very proud of both our daughters," he said quietly.

"My husband always has a good word for everyone," said Mom. "Isn't that sweet?" However, she did not make it sound like a compliment.

Mr. Marone looked rather puzzled as he said good night to Tory's parents.

Aunt Kate: I'm a very good friend of Tony Marone's. When he told me the story, I knew that Tory must have been terribly embarrassed. It's terrible to be put down in public by your mother and to have your own father embarrassed as well. But like many married couples in a troubled relationship, one partner often puts down the other. In that way, as with Myra, by damaging Trevor's image, she becomes the better person and the more important of the two. She gets the upper hand, so she thinks.

That weekend was typical of family times in the Wiley household. Mom wanted to see an art exhibit that had been advertised for weeks. Tory had assumed she would be going as well and had looked forward to it. When Saturday came, she bounded downstairs calling out, "What time are we going?"

Mom stirred her coffee. "Oh, Tory, didn't I tell you? I was only able to get two tickets, it's so crowded. So, Brenda and I are going."

"You can go, Tor," Brenda said. "I don't mind really; I'd rather see the hockey game anyway."

"No," Mom said quickly. "It's just that Brenda is so social, Tory, and there's a reception after the exhibit."

"How about the hockey game with your old dad?" her father asked.

Tory sighed but quickly smiled at her father. "Sure, Dad, I'll go with you," she said.

"Isn't that nice?" said Mom. "There, it's all settled. We each have someone to go with."

Aunt Kate: The more Myra tries to split the family in two—Brenda and her, Tory and Dad—the more eager Tory becomes to gain her mother's approval. Myra really wants to give Tory to Trevor so she will have Brenda to herself as she has always wanted. Trevor just accepts things as they are, but like other kids in a family with one overdominating parent, Tory keeps trying to win over her mother.

Things really came to a head the day my son and fiancée were coming for dinner. I just felt terrible.

David Wiley and his brand-new fiancée, Betsy, were both at school upstate. Kate had invited them, Betsy's parents, and Tory's family to dinner that weekend so everyone could met.

"We've got to get you something decent to wear," Mom told Tory a couple of days before the scheduled dinner.

Tory was thrilled. A shopping spree with her mother! She didn't even argue at the store when Myra selected a frilly pink dress that didn't suit her daughter's rather pudgy ten-year-old body at all. Tory knew she looked better in tailored clothes, but the approving look in her mother's eyes was all she wanted. When they returned home, Kate was there.

"We got Tory a dress," Mom said. "I didn't want you to be ashamed of her at the dinner party."

"That would never happen," said Aunt Kate with a wink at Tory. "How about a preview of the dress?"

"Sure." Tory ran upstairs to change. But when she looked in the mirror, she thought she resembled Miss Piggy. The frills looked awful, and she felt awkward and uncomfortable. She walked slowly downstairs, trying to be graceful and smooth.

"Well, well," said Aunt Kate.

"Stand up straight, Tory," said her mother. "You don't look comfortable at all. I don't think you want to go to the dinner party. She's not like Brenda in that way," she said to Kate. "Brenda's always so pleasant and cheerful."

"Nonsense," said Kate firmly. "Of course, Tory wants to go to the dinner party. She loves David, and he wants to see her and introduce her to Betsy. It's not the party she's uncomfortable with, it's the dress. It's not her style, Myra. Why don't you find something in your closet to wear, Tory?"

"Let's go look," said Brenda, anxious to get out of the room.

But when the two girls left the room, they stopped at the top of the stairs, knowing their mother and aunt would have something to say about the situation.

"Now look here, Myra," Kate began. "Everyone in the family knows you've always preferred Brenda, but stop making it so obvious. This is my dinner party, and I don't want any more unpleasant remarks. I will not hear another word about my lovely niece not coming to see my son."

Even though Tory had long known that Brenda was her mother's favorite, and Brenda knew it, too, it was shocking to both girls to hear it said by their aunt. Somehow that made it official. The words "everyone in the family knows you've always preferred Brenda" would remain in their ears for a long, long time.

When Tory and Brenda returned downstairs with a simpler outfit, they pretended they had overheard nothing. Tory knew it would make her aunt sad. Aunt Kate would never, never want to hurt her. The dinner party should be a happy time for Aunt Kate.

"You look great," her aunt said. "You'll be the star of the party."

Aunt Kate was wrong, of course. Nobody noticed Tory much on party night, except for David and Aunt Kate. Brenda got all the attention, but this time Tory didn't mind. For unknown to everyone, Brenda brought a date with her. She had called Aunt Kate and asked for permission just a few minutes earlier. Aunt Kate had assumed that Brenda's parents knew about it. The boy's name was Hank. He was nice enough looking, pleasant, a little uninteresting, and not overly bright. Brenda hung on his every word, but obviously her mother was less than thrilled.

At one point during the evening, Aunt Kate drew Tory aside. "Something's not quite right with you," she said, "and I have a terrible feeling it's me. You overheard what I said to your mother the other day, didn't you?"

Tory swallowed hard, but she couldn't lie to her aunt. "Yes," she said.

"I'm sorry, pet, honestly. But it's nothing you haven't thought yourself. And you have to understand that your mother grew up with a widowed mother who had a bad time making ends meet. She never knew a loving family and doesn't know how to be a truly loving mother, even though she does love you in her way. She needs help, but your parents' problems are theirs and shouldn't be yours. I'm here for you always, and I want you to remember one thing. You can't change your mother, so just be the terrific person you are. Now come help me with this terrific dessert."

The dessert *was* terrific, but the scene at the Wileys' house later wasn't. Neither was Mother's mood. For the first time that Tory could remember, Mom was furious with Brenda.

"How could you shame me like that?" she demanded. "Bringing along a boy I don't even know, and such a boy as that. I've never been so disappointed in my life."

"I didn't do anything wrong," Brenda protested. "Aunt Kate wasn't ashamed of me."

Aunt Kate: Brenda was right on that score. But I was wrong in not having paid enough attention to Brenda's problems as well as Tory's. I have two nieces and was concentrating only on one. Brenda has a problem as well. She can never live up to the image her mother created for her. Nobody is that perfect. Myra is trying to live her lost dreams through her older daughter. Besides, it's normal for teenagers to rebel. Brenda is just trying to jump down from her mother's pedestal without falling on her face.

The bickering didn't stop in the Wiley household after that. Every chance she got, Mom said something unflattering about Hank. "He's not the sort of boy you should be dating. His family is very low class, and he's obviously not very bright. You can do far better."

"Hank is a nice boy, Mom," Brenda kept saying. "I'm not marrying him for heaven's sake. I'm thirteen years old. We just go to parties and stuff. What's the big deal?"

"I don't want you to see him again," said her mother.

"That's not fair, and I'll see him if I want to," said Brenda.

Tory was shocked. She had never heard her sister defy their mother before. Maybe this was her chance. Maybe Tory could take Mom's side in this argument. Maybe now she could become Mom's favorite.

Now their mother tried another method of persuasion. "Brenda, this boy is so ordinary. He's simply not good enough for you, dear. He's not even very bright, and you have such a wonderful future ahead of you.

"Mom's right," said Tory. "Everyone knows Hank isn't the brightest guy around, Brenda, that's for sure."

"You see," their mother said. "Even your sister knows I'm right."

It was working! Mom was moving away from Brenda and toward Tory. She would win if she worked at it hard enough. But then Tory saw Brenda's eyes. The look of hurt and betrayal was shocking. She had made her sister cry.

"How can you do that?" Brenda asked. "We're sisters."

Maybe Tory could win, but what was the price? Mom's favor? Tory could never change things this way. Not really. Mom was Mom. Aunt Kate had told her that. And there was nothing anyone could do about it. Not her daughters anyway. Be the best you can be, said Aunt Kate. And the best Tory could be was herself—her best self.

"Bad joke, Brenda," Tory said, putting her arm around her sister. "Hank's okay, really. And like you said, you're not going to marry him, for heaven's sake." Tory looked at her mother. "She's only thirteen, Mom, what harm would it do to let her go to the dance?"

When her mother didn't answer right away, Tory quickly turned to Brenda. "Come on, let's go upstairs and try on clothes. No matter who you go with, everyone looks at you anyway. And Mom's right about one thing—you sure are special."

Epilogue:
Help! Where
Can You Turn?

In addition to guidance counselors, relatives, adult family friends, and clergy, listed below are some suggestions where troubled kids can find a helping hand. Following the name and address are the following keys:

A = alcohol and/or drug abuse
AD = adoption problems
C\S = child, sex abuse
G = general, multiproblem help
S = single parent family groups
SP = suicide prevention

Al-Anon Family Group Headquarters
(Al-Anon and Alateen)
1600 Corporate Landing Parkway
Virginia Beach, VA 23454–5617
(800) 344–2666
A

American Humane Society
Child Protection Division
Box 1266
Denver, CO 80201–1266
(303) 695–0811
G

Big Brothers\Big Sisters of America
2037 Chestnut Street
Philadelphia, PA 19103
(800) 767–BIG S
G

Boystown National Hotline (for girls also)
Boystown, NE
(800) 448–3000
G

Child Abuse Hotline
(800) 4ACHILD
C\S

Childhelp U.S.A.
15757 North 75th Street
Scottsdale, AZ 85260
G

Children of Alcoholics
(301) 464–2600
A

Covenant House
Crisis Center
460 West 4th Street
New York, NY 10036
(800) 999-9999
G, SP

Families Anonymous, Inc.
PO Box 3475
Culver City, CA 90231–3475
(800) 736–9805
G

Nar-Anon Family Group Headquarters
San Pedro, CA
(888) 470–7670
A

National Adoption Information Clearinghouse
PO Box 1182
Washington, DC 20013–1182
(888) 251–0075
AD

**National Center for Missing and
Exploited Children**
2101 Wilson Boulevard, Suite 550
Arlington, VA 22201–3052
(703) 235–3900
C\S, G

**National Clearinghouse on
Child Abuse and Neglect**
U.S. Department of Health and Human Services
Box 1182
Washington, DC 20013–1182
(800) FYI–3366
C\S, G

**National Committee to
Prevent Child Abuse**
Box 2866
Chicago, IL 60690
C\S

National Council on Family Relations
3989 Central Avenue NE
Minneapolis, MN 55421
(612) 781–9931
S

National Crime Prevention Council
1700 K. Street NW
Washington, DC 20006
(202) 466–6272
G

New York Society for the Prevention of Cruelty to Children (SPCC)
(212) 233–5500
C\S, G

Index

362.7
BLU
Blue, Rose

Staying out of trouble in a troubled
family

DATE DUE	BORROWER'S NAME	

362.7
BLU
Blue, Rose

Staying out of trouble in a troubled
family